Survival to Growth

Survival to Growth

Sam A. Hout

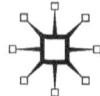

First published in 2013 by
PALGRAVE MACMILLAN®
in the United States—a division of St. Martin's Press LLC,
175 Fifth Avenue, New York, NY 10010.

Where this book is distributed in the UK, Europe and the rest of the world,
this is by Palgrave Macmillan, a division of Macmillan Publishers Limited,
registered in England, company number 785998, of Houndmills,
Basingstoke, Hampshire RG21 6XS.

Palgrave Macmillan is the global academic imprint of the above companies
and has companies and representatives throughout the world.

Palgrave® and Macmillan® are registered trademarks in the United States,
the United Kingdom, Europe and other countries.

ISBN 978-1-349-47172-0   ISBN 978-1-137-35906-3 (eBook)
DOI 10.1057/9781137359063

Library of Congress Cataloging-in-Publication Data

Hout, Sam A., 1951–
    Survival to growth / Sam A. Hout.
        pages cm

        1. Organizational change. 2. Leadership. 3. Communication in
    management. I. Title.
HD58.8.H678 2013
658.4'06—dc23   2013019247

A catalogue record of the book is available from the British Library.

Design by Newgen Knowledge Works (P) Ltd., Chennai, India.

First edition: October 2013

10 9 8 7 6 5 4 3 2 1

This book is dedicated to my ever-patient wife, Mona, my beloved daughter, Samantha, who fills me with love, and my enthusiastic son, Owen, who never fails to surprise me, whom I love very dearly. Forever, I love you all.

Contents

Figures and Tables

Figures

Tables

Preface

The main message of the book is that those who understand human nature tend to simplify methods, move fast, and provide their people with training to upgrade their skills to help them achieve business goals and objectives, that is, they instill a "Right-the-first-time culture."

"Right, the First Time" is a culture of excellence comprising a mindset, a way of acting, and a practical tool box, creating an atmosphere in which teams and individuals always perform.

Growing up in Beirut, Lebanon, was a time of either ambitious growth, or idleness due to political instability. We learned how to turn a table upside down to play billiards while gunfire was heard across the sky. We went to the movies where fictitious films appeared so real and helped in building hope and longer-term ambition that translated to goals.

During summer, I would go to the mountains and spend long hours hunting, which can be very tiring. The rewards of game pursuit brought exhaustion, but a feeling of strength following a short rest. The real excitement was in the pursuit and in the challenge of game hunting rather than in the catch. I learned that being in the game and being engaged in the goal pursuit is key to catching.

On occasions, I would fly a kite that would soar hundreds of feet high. Sometimes, the string will become entangled and I would spend a long time disentangling it patiently, and ultimately rewind the string in an orderly fashion for the next time. I started thinking how complex things might become, even if they originated in simplicity. Nonetheless, with tenaciousness, I always hoped and knew that I would disentangle the strings.

I learned chemistry and how it relates to existence and life structure. I organized information, and learned about how important mathematics is to prove concepts. In England, I formalized my technical knowledge, but more importantly learned about cultural and human interactions, and that there is room for everyone to coexist. As a young chemical engineering student, I was conducting research using a system that utilized a cooling condenser. On a very cold night, the system cooling water froze and expanded, destroying a part of the system. This setback focused my attention on lead time, which ended up with more organized experimentation, data matrix collection, data analysis and correlation, building mathematical models, and defending my thesis.

More than three decades later, in the United States, life and business experiences have solidified many concepts that I am attempting to hint at in this book.

The druthers in this book are to focus on the future and on accomplishments, and provide for timeless experiences.

"Our Problems cannot be solved at the same level of thinking that created them," said Albert Einstein.

John F. "Jack" Welch Jr. promoted decision-focused "workouts" to solve problems, championed six sigma methodologies, periodically evaluated executive performance, and sent the bottom 10 percent packing. He insisted that if a business was not number one or number two in its market, it should be fixed, sold, or closed. Powerful among the thinkers is Eliyahu M. Goldratt, an unconstrained idea-man, whose theory of constraints helped manufacturers remove broken links from their value chain and improve performance.

Andrew S. Grove, former CEO, Intel, asserted highly that only the paranoid survive. On the other hand, Michael Dell, CEO of the eponymous computer firm, crafted a new kind of supply chain and launched a revolutionary business model, an Internet-based business approach to purchasing, mass customization, and remarkable after-sale services.

Management guru Peter Drucker's basic message is that people are the most important asset of a company, and the management's obligation is to provide people the freedom to perform. W. Edwards Deming, with focus on statistical quality control, and Joseph J. Juran, with emphasis on the "internal customer," who highlighted the importance of total quality control as a management tool for improving the quality of products and services, have been among the most recognized quality-process thinkers of the past three decades.

Oracle chairman Larry Ellison, Microsoft Corporation chairman Bill Gates, Seibel Systems founder Tom Seibel, and SAS Inc. CEO James Goodnight are four combination thinkers and doers as knowledge managers have provided the tools that allow people to take control of complex manufacturing and services operations.

The late Eli Hurvitz, former board chairman of Teva Pharmaceuticals, highlighted the major risks that any company could face:

1. Arrogance: "Never, ever be arrogant. It prevents people (and companies) from seeing the basic truth."
2. Bureaucracy: "Without process you cannot execute the content, but companies—regardless of their size—often forget about the content."
3. Lack of Focus: "Strategy should be clear, understood by everyone. And everyone, from the board of directors to every level of management, should know exactly what they are doing."

He insisted that the chairperson and the CEO must be different people to clearly distinguish their roles. "There must be a clear distinction between the two functions." The CEO should be involved more directly in the hands-on day-to-day operations while the chairman should focus more on the macro-decisions. He used to joke with the board when he was CEO that his responsibility is to make money, and their responsibility was to decide what to do with it. In a way, that is really the essence of each role; "What to do" is about the macro, and the board is responsible for the strategic decisions—where to invest, whether to acquire a company, open another business, sell a business, pay dividends, to contribute, and so on. Moreover, while they are all very important business issues, they also embody a cultural element. They deal with the company and its environment—How does the company want to interact with the community?

Acknowledgments

In this book effort there were many moments where I needed to stop to think about the impact of a particular section or concept, and the contributors. However, I am indebted to the professional efforts of Nancy Rosenfeld for her pursuit of excellence in guiding this write-up to publication. Her vision, detail orientation, and hard work in leading this effort are greatly appreciated. I am also grateful to my friend and colleague Ron Momtahan for his continuous support and guidance in providing for technical input on graphics and computer related issues without which these tasks would not have materialized.

1

Survival: Simple, Curious, and Interested

Keep it simple. Ask the right questions. Move fast. Learn. Get it done. Being an expert in international trade is different from possessing expertise in design or in some other trade, and yet similarities exist that we can compare. It is important to define the elements we are seeking. Focusing on individuals in the selection process is a key factor in how the future can be shaped. First, we need to analyze the job and the people to be trained: We should ask what people need to know to perform well on the job. How much relevant prior knowledge do they each have? What is each person's motivation? What is the perceived value of their training?

Each job description comprises its own set of requirements in terms of knowledge, skill, and level of ability. Since we document knowledge in terms of concepts, principles, procedures, and examples that address issues at hand, how then do we raise intellectual capital?

In terms of the mechanisms that will support and demonstrate our goals and objectives, how do we transfer technology? Moreover, what practice and feedback procedures are to be employed and what questions remain? How do we conduct an evaluation of design and an effective business plan? Finally, how do we carry the message in terms of media selection: live, Web-based, or video?

The answer is a natural selection—a gradual, nonrandom process by which traits become more or less common as a function of differential characteristics over time and exhibit variability. Variation exists within every process. This occurs partly because random causes of change can occur, but they can also be normalized and controlled. Throughout the process of personal interactions within a specific environment, causes of variations are observed. This includes individuals who possess certain variants of traits, some of whom may survive and produce more than individuals with other variants. It becomes an evolving process of selectivity, the strongest of whom will survive and flourish.

Observable characteristics in each individual offer productive advantages that become more apparent over time in a particular group or population. This process can result in groups of people who specialize in a particular niche, and which may eventually end in the emergence of an entirely new method or system. In natural selection, the environment acts as a sieve through which only certain variations can pass.

Natural variation occurs among individuals of all groups of people, and, in many instances, these differences do not affect survival (such as differences in eye color). Conversely, some differences may improve an individual's chance of survival. Take, for example, a rabbit that runs faster than others and may be more likely to escape its predators. Likewise, the individual (or company) with stronger qualifications will surpass their contenders in tasks that places them ahead of those competing for the same or similar positions. Just as algae, which are more efficient at extracting energy from sunlight, grow faster than plants of the same species that are less energy efficient. Whatever increases the chances of an individual's survival also affects their rate of productivity. Although sometimes there's a trade-off between survival and current production, what matters ultimately is the total lifetime production of the individual. Therefore, natural selection appears to be the most important mechanism for creating complex adaptations.

The comparison between political and emotional intelligence team leaders is meant to focus on the realities of these behavioral approaches insisting upon a particular approach as the correct one. It is merely meant to reflect on observations of two different styles of management that are practiced in organizations. Some of the greatest intimidators that face a team organizer or sponsor are based on subtle observations. We hear a lot of praise for emotionally intelligent, even humble, leaders. Nevertheless, change is perceived by some followers as scary, and followers sometimes appear to respond to scary leaders to steer them through the issues. Those with bold political intelligence can creatively push followers to excel in their performance. Therefore, team initiators need to do their homework. They appear to work harder and tend to laugh at the team members' antics. By earning members' respect and calling their bluff, they ensure keeping their perspective and commitment to sticking around. While leaders with social intelligence use empathy and soft power to build bridges, politically intelligent leaders use intimidation and hard power to exploit the anxieties and vulnerabilities they detect.

The selection of how and what kinds of teams are developed within an organization will determine the level of success and health of a company. Traditionally, many organizations selected teams based on employees' availability, emphasizing credulity, ensuring consensus, and trumping creativity in favor of efficiency with a focus on reaching the average customer base. On the other hand, adept organizations might focus their teams on skill, innovation, and sophistication, targeting select or maybe elite customers. Tables 1.1 and 1.2 illustrate these two team concepts: curiosity to know and constant search for excellence.

Table 1.1 Teams' Selectivity

Traditional Teams	Virtuoso Teams

1. Choose members for availability
  • Assign members according to individual availability and past experience with the problem
  • Fill in the team as needed
	1. Choose members for skills
	  • Insist on hiring those with the best skills, regardless of the individuals' familiarity with the problem
	  • Recruit specialists for each position in the team

2. Emphasize the collective
  • Repress individual egos
  • Encourage members to get along
  • Choose a solution based on consensus
  • Assure that efficiency trumps creativity
	2. Emphasize the individual
	  • Celebrate individual egos and elicit the best from each team member
	  • Encourage members to compete and create opportunities for solo performances
	  • Choose a solution based on merit
	  • Assure that creativity trumps efficiency

3. Focus on tasks
  • Complete critical tasks on time
  • Get the project done on time
	3. Focus on ideas
	  • Generate a rich and frequent flow of ideas among team members
	  • Find and express the breakthrough idea on time

4. Work individually and remotely
  • Require individual members to complete tasks on their own
  • Allow communication via e-mail, phone, and weekly meetings
  • Encourage polite conversations
	4. Work together and intensively
	  • Force members into close physical proximity
	  • Force members to work together at a fast pace
	  • Force direct dialogue without sparing feelings

5. Address the average customer
  • Attempt to reach the broadest possible customer base; appeal to the average
  • Base decisions on established market knowledge
  • Affirm common stereotypes
	5. Address the sophisticated customer
	  • Attempt to surprise customers by stretching their expectations; appeal to the sophisticate
	  • Defy established market knowledge
	  • Reject common stereotypes

Table 1.2 Types of Organization

Healthy	Unhealthy

1. Resilient
  • Highly adaptable to external market shifts
  • Focused on and aligned behind a coherent business strategy
	1. Passive–Aggressive
	  • Congenial / lacks candor
	  • Seemingly conflict-free
	  • Achieves consensus easily
	  • Struggles in implementation of agreed-upon plans

2. Just-in-time
  • Prepared for change
  • Can rise to unanticipated challenge
  • Does not lose sight of the big picture
	2. Over-managed
	  • Multi layers of management
	  • Analysis-paralysis scenarios
	  • Politicized decision making

3. Military precision
  • Small involved senior team
  • Success is determined through superior execution
  • Effective operating model
	3. Outgrown
	  • Too large and complex ineffective structure
	  • Complicated systems that cannot be controlled by a small team
	  • Democratized decision-making authority

	4. Fits and starts
	  • Too many mavericks that are not aligned
	  • Scores of smart talented people who are not team players

Regardless of how a specific industry is trending, a company might be doing great because of its own behavior. On the other hand, if an employee's healthy impulses to learn and share, and to achieve, are not encouraged, damaging adaptive conduct will gradually take over. Misunderstandings, and misrepresentation, about who has control over decisions are frequently the first signs that an organization is slipping into passive–aggressive territory.

Scanning the Periphery

As organizations build their marketing campaigns to meet customer requirements by creating an edge to their products and services, they also must remain alert through competitor analysis and to survey the different fronts on which they are competing in the market place. Therefore, scanning the periphery of their operations and the scope of their work is imperative to their future continuity and survival. The following will illustrate the significance of keeping an eye on competition.

When an order from the top management is necessary to organize for scanning the periphery, whose responsibility is it to question the authority of such a mandate? As part of the organization, an effort is made to assign accountability to an existing functional group, such as corporate development, competitor intelligence, market research, or technology forecasting. However, assigning a midlevel group is not risk-free. Especially, if the assigned groups limit themselves to their usual resources, using data from domains they know rather than scanning broadly and conveying to others about what they have learned. The overseer might want to mobilize ad hoc issue groups to assure the level of data collection, and then a management committee can identify the most important questions. Separate task forces should be enforced to pursue each question. This process would establish a scenario analysis to identify key uncertainties that would be studied and monitored to create a high-level lookout. The management committee would have the responsibility of putting a team in place to scan topics, such as customer diversity and collaborative networks at the periphery. This team should rise above all functional and product blinders while the team leader shares his insights with the top management. They are the ones who act as lookouts for new discoveries and dangerous liaisons.

Before embarking on any new initiative, the management committee focuses its attention on the periphery (e.g., Royal Dutch-Shell Game Changer program, 1996). It charters to envision and test its hypotheses regarding new opportunities beyond the core, and then screens ideas and identifies technologies before getting to work on them. These technologies would be commercialized and new businesses created. Next, the management committee would recommend investing in start-up ventures, or pool capital to invest in start-ups. The investments might be modest, but would open a clear window of prospective emerging technology and new markets. A management committee might subcontract by employing consultants, who would be responsible for predicting the factors needed to transform a business and incorporate the insights of these "private eyes" into strategic decision making.

"Extraordinary insights often come from uncommon perspectives"

—Harvard Business Review, November 2005.

Go on. Be a tiger!

2

Leadership? Who?

Humility and willpower shape the highest-level leader. According to Jim Collins, in his book *Good to Great: Why Some Companies Make the Leap...and Others Don't*, good leadership is determined by the person who attends to the people first and strategy second. "Get the right people on the bus, move the wrong people off," says Collins. "Usher the right people to the right seats. Figure out where to drive the bus."

According to Collins (2001), top-level leaders possess the following attributes: personal humility and professional will. Personal humility is a consistent demonstration of a compelling modesty, which always comes across as natural and never boastful. This type of leader always acts with a quiet, calm determination. He/she relies principally on standards, and not charisma, to influence stakeholders. These leaders focus on ambition for the goodwill of the company's longer-term goals and growth.

On the other hand, the professional will displayed by these leaders focuses on results irrespective of challenges to emphasize longer-term gains. Always acknowledge others along the road of achievements; never apportion blame, external factors, or bad luck!

Since the essence of self-management is controlling, providing employees the opportunity to control their own jobs, self-efficacy is a critical link in making self-management work. From a leadership perspective, it refers enhancing individual and team self-efficacy. Self-management is defined here as the set of strategies a person uses to influence and convert perceived obstacles into opportunities. Ultimately, the term "super leadership" describes the process of directing others to lead themselves.

Conscious use of positive models, setting goals focused on employee self-development, encouragement from the leader, guidance for exercising self-leadership, and appropriate rewards/reprimands are key factors in developing super leadership. The new leadership paradigm emerges in finding a balance of cognitive–behavioral perspectives. Managers act to ensure a positive influence on employee behavior. In addition, a manager attempts to influence the employee's pattern of thought (emphasis on cognition).

Leadership theory, which is based on trait, behavioral approach, the contingency model, and the shift to transactional and transformational leadership, is all about influencing others. The act of motivating and influencing others is illustrated through the following styles of leadership:

1. strong man, typifying a physical characteristic-based model;
2. behavior of a trans-actor corresponding to reinforcement and goal-setting approach in which the leader evokes performance by using variations of the carrot-and-stick model of professional management;
3. the visionary hero: here, followers are primarily dependent on the leader through inspiration and vision;
4. super leader: guides his employees to lead themselves.

In comparison, the super leader emphasizes building self-efficacy on the part of followers. Super leadership emphasizes teamwork, initiating self-managed teams, and super leadership is the applied manifestation of social cognitive theory.

For example, contingent reward is an important part of super leadership, especially when reinforcing self-leadership to their followers; and, goal setting—based on strong self-efficacy—is perhaps the single most important ingredient for followers to learn from super leadership.

The pragmatic prioritization of how to succeed in influencing others can best be determined by a leader who can establish a vision and overall direction by entertaining long-term decision making in regard to the domain in which the organization competes. Goals would be consistent with the overall direction—written, specific, challenging, and yet realistic and measurable. Employees are reinforced for good performance, and their managers—when necessary—are authorized to employ the use of constructive contingent reprimands. In addition, they need to be able to manage and facilitate change as the field evolves with newer and better technology. The challenge for the management rests on their ability to enhance their employees' sense of self-efficacy, create positive mental attitudes, and teach them how to accept mistakes as learning opportunities rather than failures.

Our position in creating an environment of super leadership is based on mastering and modeling self-leadership as a set of skills for effectively influencing our own behavior and thinking. This is the key component to achieving the level of high performance for which we aspire. The most dramatic results of super leadership are realized through the transition of followers to self-leadership.

Yoshio Ishizaka, president and CEO of Toyota Motor Corporation, has developed eight rules of leadership during his 40 plus years with Toyota:

1. Have an open mind and a love of travel.
2. Good leaders communicate as much by hearing as they do by talking.

3. Good leaders pack a positive attitude.
4. Good leaders invest in their minds and bodies.
5. To be a good leader you must remain a student for life.
6. A good leader respects others at all levels.
7. True leaders believe in building an entire team.
8. Good leaders know how to have fun.

In today's highly competitive and challenging work environment, managing employees to increase and sustain gains of performance requires that both self-efficacy and leadership go hand in hand. The effectiveness of self-efficacy, in conjunction with super leadership, enhances employee performance while motivating them to achieve their goals in the context of specific task accomplishments. Classification of self-efficacy / super leadership attributes was highlighted and underscored as a major approach to managing employee performance. Therefore, conceptual theory and practical implications of self-efficacy / super leadership should be the focus of continuous training, which is the yardstick for measuring performance standards. The emphasis on improving employee self-efficacy and setting specific goals is suggested in the process of obtaining goal acceptance in a participative environment. This will increase an employee's knowledge about the tasks at hand while creating a sense of control to ensure the commitment to goals and the ability to meet objectives.

Successful leadership will have a major effect on the motives and preferences of their employees, as well as determining future goals and their ultimate commitment to the complex structure of the organization. The successful leadership of a corporation can even be compared with the performance of the presidential office in Washington. A president's success is gauged by the strength of the nation's economy, the number of bills that successfully pass through Congress, and by public opinion. A strong, successful president understands the needs and expectations of his constituents, and has the ability to lead the country in the right direction to achieve the shared end values of the American people. Outstanding leadership is measured by a leader's ability to share a common vision with the public in an assertive, oratorical manner that also reaches a high degree of emotional nonverbal expression. Messages can be effectively delivered by communicating in a mild yet deliberate and soft-spoken manner. Besides vision, a good president projects passion and self-sacrifice in serving the public whose confidence must be earned. With determination, persistence, and by surrounding himself with likable and strong role models for key presidential positions, the image of the president gradually evolves and builds over time. Selective motivation on major events is critical to the mission of the president. Frame alignment, which is a broad theoretical approach of communication used for persuading followers to accept and implement change, was specifically practiced by Presidents Roosevelt, Kennedy, Reagan, and Clinton. Each invoked inclusive terms of distant goals that inspired a common vision for the future.

Although the president of the United States is frequently regarded as the most powerful person on earth, he remains accountable to the American public. If the economy turns south for an extended period of time, the public elects a different president. The source of power of the presidency is the inspirational message that is conveyed and chartered throughout his programs. The president defines the direction of how he envisions his cabinet to execute the programs, which are aligned with the overall concepts and philosophies of his presidency (his vision).

As long as the American people believe that the country is moving in the right direction (in their favor), they will continue to back the president's vision irrespective of how he may actually be discharging his duties. Difficult relationships with the legislative arms of government, and the court system, as we have witnessed in the case of President Clinton, did not change the support of the American people for him as they felt that they were doing better irrespective of the president's legal issues (he was reelected to the presidency).

Super leadership is the participative sharing of responsibility and authority. Conversely, the presidential source of power is the inspirational content of what he projects based on his vision. All sources of direction are carefully chartered by leaders, but it is the super leaders who are capable of eliciting their followers to help in providing a new course of direction. However, it is up to the president to carefully review all suggestions before determining the right course of action that the White House will pursue.

When followers respond to strong leadership, their reaction tends to be compliance based on fear. The super leader followers have an emotional commitment to their leader and a vested interest based on shared ownership. For the presidency, the American people stand behind their leader in a show of emotional commitment grounded on the president's vision.

Since the focus of American society is on the presidency rather than on the Supreme Court or the joint houses of Congress, Americans want a leader who shares their vision and is someone with whom they can connect with emotionally. Although we understand the importance of the checks-and-balances system within our three branches of government, it is the office of the president that remains first and foremost for the American people.

Although leadership produces strong differences among its followers, it can be transformational, effective, or participative. Leaders can also possess all these characteristics in various proportions. A visionary leader, for example, Alexander, who was the disciple of Aristotle, could both administer and execute.

Table 2.1 Leadership Traits

Leadership attribute	Value-adding behavior	Leadership attribute	Value-adding behavior
Intense desire to lead	Self-reliance	Cooperative	Identify key people
	In control		Build relationships
	Autonomous		Manage power
	Motivated followers		Manage dependencies
	High self-esteem		Build consensus
	Positive image		
	Dreamer	Communicator	Clarity
	Self-motivator		Define contribution
			Helpful
Express purpose	Provide significance		Define expectations
	Highlight value		Low pressure on selling
	Make customer central focus		Negotiator
			Seeks compromise
Visible	Always in field		
	Manage by walking around	Excellent listener	Attentive
			No interruption
Build winning teams	Coach team		Listen to learn
	Develop people		
	Plan	Self-efficacy	Aware
	Get the facts		Sensitive
	Fallback plan		Task excellence
	Selective player assignments		Honest / high integrity
	Weed out incompetence		Command
	Open communications		Consult
	Free flow of information		
	Commitment to excellence	Grow and develop	Read
			Study
	High ticket items		Seek advice
	Profit		Ask
	High profit		Build on strength
	Build trust		Compensate weakness
	Reliable		

In developing a sense of mission based on defined goals, the success of your leadership rests on your best level of performance, your sense of direction, and your ability to unite others along a common path while maintaining your honesty and integrity—the key attributes to good leadership. This is combined with action orientation based on innovation, an entrepreneurial spirit, forward thinking, and the pragmatic ability to "do," "try," and "fix."

Moments of decision making require decisive and courageous leadership, a person capable of performing with boldness, audacity, and one who has the ability to create hope and positive thinking with a can-do attitude. This is a leader who remains the driving force of all operations on his watch, and is motivated to keep moving forward. He initiates action, defines the angles of attack, and knows how to stay the course while defining the level of risk.

As leaders work with their team to characterize a clear strategy that reflects on big-picture events and processes, they follow methodical and logical systematic procedures focused on strength and the ability to react quickly under stress. This is mandatory to avoid mishaps from occurring due to any unavoidable, or unforeseen, weakness in the system. In addition, a good leader builds trust and inspires the confidence and loyalty of his teammates by his ability to delegate by empowering and encouraging his followers (see table 2.1).

Although good leaders also need to accept, and to benefit from, any accidental failure that everyone at all levels of an organization experiences at one time or another, they should never deter from accomplishing their task at hand nor lose sight of their ultimate goal. The road to victory is always paved with stones, and with new opportunities around the corner. Winning remains the overall objective.

3

It Is the How?

How can companies sustain success by injecting certain behaviors from the beginning?

How do you convert companies and performances to achieve best results?

How do we differentiate high-performing companies from average?

Learn from the people. Plan with the people... When the task is accomplished, the people will acknowledge the remark: "We have done it ourselves." For example, the asthma drug Xolair was presented as an infusion drug, similar to cancer treatment drugs, to the physicians specialized in asthma treatment, without any initial training, even though they were not familiar with the intricate procedures that are not common to this discipline. People are much more likely to act their way into a new way of thinking, than to think their way into a new way of acting.

A manager gets results by working with others. A superior manager gets superior results by working with people. Keep your eye on the ball. Ask, why are you on the payroll? Look for measurable results and unique contribution. Think, what are we trying to do? How are we doing it? Focus on key results area in terms of customers' needs, economic difficulties, quality, productivity, innovation, people growth, and organizational development.

Define standards of performance by assigning specific measurable timing, basis for rewards, and quality control (inspect what you expect). Monitor for concentration of power in critical areas.

Effective delegation by matching skills to tasks, explaining expected results (Why? How?), defining preferred method of approach, and assigning 100 percent responsibility will increase the chances of success of a task. Nonetheless, it is important to resist temptation to interfere, but it is also important to create key performance climate through a stretch challenge, respecting opinions, and providing for positive confident expectation. Removing obstacles by limiting steps in the process and defining critical path items is key to achieving milestones. Parallel to delegation, a supervisor also needs to carefully swarm all over without being in the way.

Excellence in Ethics

Shouldn't we find significance in our work and the opportunity to use our mind and feeling while appealing to the animating or life-giving principles within us? Bill George, former CEO of Medtronic, asks: "Man (Woman) must strive to live a full life. An unwavering devotion to the highest possible legal, moral, and ethical standards should be at the heart of team efforts. With the emphasis on cost controls, there is a very strong temptation to manage strictly by the numbers and ignoring other ethical factors. It is important to highlight ethical context in clear company main objectives and declared mission. A pursuit of an effort to maintain this mission and vision in a highly quantified environment should never curtail ethical and integrity statements and actions." This ethical attitude should be a testament to company leadership as an unsurpassed standard of comparison and recognition of dedication to conducting business in an honest manner and serve as an example of integrity.

Table 3.1   Communications—the Four Agreements

Be impeccable with your word

Speak with integrity. Say only what you mean. Avoid using the word to speak against yourself or to gossip about others. Use the power of your word in the direction of truth and empathy. Be Positive.

Don't make assumptions

Find the courage to ask questions and to express what you really want. Communicate with others as clearly as you can to avoid misunderstandings, sadness, and drama. With just this one agreement, you can transform your communications skills.

Don't take anything personally

Nothing others do is because of you. What others say and do is a projection of their own reality, their own dream. When you are immune to the opinions of others you won't be the victim of needless suffering.

Always do your best

Your best is going to change from moment to moment. It will be different when you are healthy as opposed to sick. Under any circumstance, simply do your best and avoid self-judgment, self-abuse, and regret.

A compliance program should be designed to ensure that every employee lives up to the key corporate policy emphasizing legal and ethical standards of conduct. Team members must strive to flush out ethical issues and bring them out in the open without any fear of reprisal. Codes of conduct must be enforced with the utmost urgency by the executive committee. Initiatives to spread this behavior should be based on cooperation and partnerships with the suppliers and customers across the globe. Table 3.1 summarizes communication values that will enhance and guarantee cooperation among both internal and external customers and suppliers.

Listening Skills

In my judgment, the most important skill that leaders must master is the "listening skill," without which managers will fail in achieving their goals, and relationships will suffer detrimental consequences, including personal ones. The primary goal of listening is to allow an individual to express his/her feelings and resolve his/her own problems. The listener achieves this by: (1) validating feelings and problems, (2) clarifying and identifying needs, (3) exploring options, and (4) sharing communication skills. Preparation for listening requires relaxation or "quieting the mind" in order to provide undivided attention to the other person without interruption.

The focus is on feelings, paying attention to visual and vocal cues, and matching your tone to the speaker's. The effective listener hears more than the speaker's words. One listens to the pitch, rate, timbre, and other subtle nuances of voice that communicate meaning. Feelings like anger, enthusiasm, and joy are accompanied by increased rate of speech, higher volume, and higher pitch. A slower-than-normal rate, lower volume, and lower pitch tend to characterize feelings of boredom or depression. Observe the speaker's body language and attempt to keep your body in a neutral, relaxed position. Your "quiet" body can have a calming effect, place the speaker at ease, and help build trust.

Reflective listening is simply repeating, restating, or clarifying what the speaker has just said. Sometimes it is just putting words to the emotions you hear the speaker express: "You sound upset." Reflective listening lets the speaker know you are staying with him or her. It is a good opportunity to check back and see if what you think you heard is what the person actually said or meant. Don't plan what you will say next…rather, really listen and reflect back and summarize. A technique that complements listening is called the "verbal nod." It is a way of connecting by saying, "uh-huh," "yes," "oh," or "I see." This lets the speaker know you are listening and focused on what he/she is telling you. It is important not to say, "I know just how you feel," or "I really understand," because no one knows exactly how another person feels.

Nonjudgmental listening is essential. Make every effort to refrain from jumping to conclusions about whether you agree or disagree with the speaker. Acceptance validates the speaker and helps to establish a good relationship. Otherwise, you may cut off communication. No matter how much you disagree with or are emotionally affected by what you're hearing, it is important to remain calm and open-minded. Your biases may hinder your ability to listen effectively. It is never a listener's place to argue or educate. Avoid imposing your beliefs, giving advice, reassuring unknowingly, and offering solutions.

Avoid the solution syndrome, that is, don't give advice or offer solutions. The focus is to assist the speaker to explore and clarify his/her feelings and needs. This support encourages the person to feel empowered and enables him/her to come to his/her own conclusions. By being supportive and giving feedback, you enable the speaker to succeed in finding his/her own solutions. This encourages efficient problem solving and increases the individual's sense of control.

Ask appropriate questions. Make statements to help the speaker assess the situation and feel supported and listened to. It is inappropriate to interrogate, but thoughtful questions help the speaker clarify the situation and needs. Open-ended questions are particularly useful in eliciting more information:

Is there something you would like to talk about?

Where would you like to begin?

Can you tell me more?

How do you feel about that?

It sounds like this is really hard for you to talk about.

Who else knows about this?

Have you considered what options you have?

Concentrate/focus on what the speaker is saying, that is, "stay with" the person. Avoid drifting along and coming across as uninterested or unfocused. Your ability to respond sincerely sends a message of caring to the speaker. Your empathy and attention may be one of the catalysts to empower the speaker to better understand and confront issues.

Silence is golden. Occasionally, a speaker may pause. The person may need a moment to collect his/her thoughts and decide what to say next. Allowing silence is necessary to effective listening. Your silence demonstrates your willingness to go at the speaker's pace, in an unhurried fashion. A gentle reassurance that you're still listening may be helpful during a long pause.

Encourage the person to expand his/her options and support network. What has helped in the past? Who can assist the speaker (family, friends, groups, church, pets, etc.)? Provide referrals for additional support, if appropriate.

Technology

The use of technology as a tool to accelerate momentum to create processes that present advantages in customer contacts, relations, and sales and advance operational effectiveness is one investment that a company has to assess carefully. Choices should focus on presenting an advantage of convenience as well as cost to the customer, for instance, bar code scanners, inventory management, invoicing, inter-country trade forms (e.g., NAFTA requirements), etc.

Technologies such as computer-aided design / drafting (CAD) and interactive inventory tracking, including geographical spread with continuous tracking, play a major role in building the technological framework in a company. Sophisticated algorithms, mathematical models to assess economic factors and risk management, apply to manufacturing technology and cash flow cycle. Building management systems utilizing programmable logic controllers (PLC) and supervisory control and data acquisition (SCADA) systems are key introductions to modernization and automation.

Laboratory testing with upgraded instruments and documenting results using a laboratory instruments and management system (LIMS) increase compliance and accuracy in a well-organized automated tracking system.

The use of statistical process control (SPC) will enhance quality assurance by using systematic methodologies and improved communications. Customer relationships management (CRM) that categorizes information in database management and networking enterprise resource planner will enhance a company's effort to build knowledge management expert systems. Hence, it is important to maintain a balanced perspective on technology. Look at it as a process accelerator rather than a primary cause of success. Thoughtless reliance on technology might be more of a liability than an asset. Technology must fit the overall strategy.

Guidance Transcript to a Model Company

When I accepted to undertake the role to lead in developing this company model, I wanted to project to the company stakeholders that the company vision would be transparent in its communications and display discipline in its decision making. Our intent was to model an unrivaled company, set the standard for a new model in the specific industry, and successfully address the needs of customers, while providing for significant shareholder return. Table 3.2 demonstrates the approaches to change management.

The leadership team should take a hard look at all aspects of the business. They should project having a solid company, excellent potential, a robust set of opportunities, and a very promising

Table 3.2 Change Management

Traditional approach to change	Positive approach to change
1. Leadership as path breakers • Top down momentum	1. Leadership as inquiry • Leaders ask questions • Leaders facilitate search • Community takes ownership • Participants champion the quest for change
2. Outside In • Experts/consultants identify and disseminate best practices	2. Inside Out • Community identifies preexisting solutions and amplifies them
3. Deficit-based • Leaders deconstruct common problems/approach/solutions • Consultants recommend best practice based on outside experiences • Implications: people start pointing fingers • Leaders start asking questions based on comparing people rather than individual capacities: for example, "Why aren't you as good as your peers?"	3. Asset-based • Community leverages preexisting solutions practiced by those who succeed against the odds
4. Logic-driven • Participants think into new way of acting	4. Learning-driven • Participants act into a new way of thinking
5. Vulnerable to transplant rejection • Resistance arises from ideas imported or imposed by outsiders	5. Open to self-replication • Latent wisdom is tapped within a community to circumvent the social system's reaction
6. Flows from problem solving to solution identification • Best practices are applied to problems defined within the context of existing parameters	6. Flows from solution identification to process problem solving • Solution space is expanded through the discovery of new parameters
7. Focused on the protagonists • Engages stakeholders who would be conventionally associated with the problem	7. Focused on enlarging the network • Identifies stakeholders beyond those directly involved with the problem

future based on goodwill. In addition, the executive leadership team should complete a strategic business plan and outline the following year's financial plan. The leadership team should have a thorough understanding of the elements of business and draw a clear line based on the past trajectory of the company performance's key operating indicators. With that in hand, the stakeholders will have a clear insight into commitments to execute on a strategy to reshape and enhance the company's future.

The leadership team needs to review all historical transactions and efforts to strengthen the business pipeline, expand manufacturing or services, and secure leadership by value and volume in global markets. These transactions complement the existing business strategy and fuel growth. The company should evaluate outstanding core business in many countries, and focus on exceptional portfolio and an excellent industrial and geographic reach, which provide a base that few have accomplished. This is the base that the company builds on.

The company should measure investor confidence to ensure that it does not diminish. The goal is to improve the company's performance, clearly to demonstrate that it is in a unique position, and continue to better investor confidence.

As part of that process, the leadership team needs to commit itself not only to consistent performance and reliability, but also to show greater transparency and allow the investment community to better understand the company business. Presently, while the leadership team understands that the financial outlook presented may differ from what is being anticipated, it should also assure stakeholders that the management team is devoted to carefully laying out financial performance in a manner that is clear, precise, credible, and achievable. The leadership team must demonstrate that they are taking steps to do just that.

The leadership team will present guidance for the next year's main core business and other specialties. It should project product sales and services based on conservative estimates in every business sector and region. Product sales should be projected to increase or decrease by a certain amount based on estimates and the same should be justified. The projected growth in the sales of other products should be in specific categories. The leadership team should expand commitment to products in the future based on the greatest value.

The leadership team should highlight mainstream businesses. Business projections should be based on a solid business with excellent fundamentals and a good opportunity for improvement and growth, in addition to market potential upsides, and the potential for additional competition, as main thrusts. The leadership team should be working hard to drive the business, and, as the core manufacturer, should be committed to assuring the customer base.

The leadership team should anticipate global main product sales valuation, taking into consideration the introduction of new products, the market dynamics and pending regulatory concerns, and sources of variability. Market penetration of any of these products will depend crucially on the regulatory assessment of potential issues. The business must express commitment to continue to deliver the safety and efficacy of products. Specific examples that demonstrate product efficacy and safety must be cited. Specialty product projections should be estimated and declared. Expected sales of growth projects should be identified. Sales and marketing expenses should be projected as part of the percentage of sales. All royalties and additional expenses for prelaunch marketing activities should be accounted for. These investments are an important part of driving growth. The leadership team should have confidence that these investments will steer the business upward.

We turn now to another aspect of a company's business, R&D. While the leadership team makes R&D a priority, they also use a disciplined approach to discontinue some of the subsistent R&D programs, which are noncomplementary to the company's future focus. The leadership team should ensure that the R&D is of world-class standards,, focusing on specialized areas, complex mainstream products, and areas that hold greater promise.

As the company discontinues some of the legacy programs, it could choose to enhance R&D on select and targeted business development efforts. This reflects on the commitment to build both an organic and licensing pipeline, which is paramount to a future and a successful product enterprise and leads to increased shareholder value. The leadership team must continue to show commitment to full transparency and provide for greater insight on how they think about the fundamentals of the company business. They should always be ready to provide additional guidance and greater details as they go forward. The intent is to enhance the company's competitive position through strategic opportunities with the goal of creating a dynamic company that encompasses the best of capabilities in its present day, and delivers the highest quality, value products, and services in the future. This future is focused on innovation, an ongoing commitment to assembling a superior management team, highly targeted business development efforts, and a disciplined, but aggressive approach to seeking growth opportunities while maximizing profitability. These efforts should be coupled with deep attention to serving the needs of customers, working on partnerships, and creating value for shareholders. As Dr. Jeremy Levin, CEO, Teva pharmaceuticals,stated: "Greatness cannot be only 'saving' or 'spending,' there must also be vision, leadership, strategic execution with a focus on resource allocation, creativity, applied to the pipeline development and highly targeted and strategically focused business development." Table 3.3 highlights the main aspects in product development.

Table 3.3   Management Principles of Product Development System

1. *Establish*
   - Customer-defined value
   - Separate value-added activity from waste
2. *Front-Load*
   - Product development process while there is maximum design space
   - Explore alternate solutions thoroughly
3. *Create*
   - Leveled product development process flow
4. *Utilize*
   - Rigorous standardization to reduce variation
   - Create flexibility and predictable outcomes
5. *Develop*
   - Chief engineer system to integrate development from start to finish
   - Towering technical competence in all engineers
6. *Organize*
   - To balance functional expertise and cross-functional integration
7. *Integrate*
   - Supplier into the product development system
8. *Build*
   - Learning and continuous improvement
   - Culture of excellence and relentless improvement
9. *Adapt*
   - Technology to fit your people and process
10. *Align*
    - Organization through simple visual communication
11. *Use*
    - Powerful tools for standardization and organizational learning

Core Competencies

The assessment of a model employee targets the individual's understanding of competency and its associated behaviors. He/she consistently demonstrates these behaviors in a way that far exceeds the expectations of performance for these competencies, and can be viewed as a role model/mentor for the behaviors. He/she inspires others to perform at higher levels or to exceed expectations. These efforts and contributions are significantly greater than the general expectations of the role and are considered a significant strength for the individual. He/she demonstrates understanding of the business environment, internal and external factors, and seeks opportunities to improve relationships, products, or services. These are considered talents possessed by the individual.

Excellence in Execution

The team focus should be on ensuring best in class performance and continuous improvement in all areas. They can inspire others to achieve outstanding results by ensuring that each individual

- demonstrates resourcefulness and initiative and creates an appropriate level of urgency to meet objectives and deadlines;
- promotes quality and safety practices in line with the company's key values and mindset;
- effectively utilizes and prioritizes all resources and technologies required to get the job done;
- drives consistently for higher performance. Sets ambitious goals. Executes with the ability to be agile and flexible even under adverse circumstances;
- introduces incremental improvements to enhance business performance;
- demonstrates a thorough understanding of, and adheres to, the company's code of conduct policy;
- recognizes and respects confidentiality of information and uses discretion in discussing issues with others; and
- transforms company's values into actions.

Customer Orientation

The team establishes and maintains effective relationships with customers and gains their trust and respect. It

- establishes long-term relationship with customers based on integrity and trust;

- drives to secure best in class service; and
- actively seeks and includes customer feedback and perspective in our thinking and approaches.

Strategic Vision

An individual in this category articulates a clear and compelling vision and translates strategy into a road map for success. This individual

- communicates a compelling and inspired vision;
- sets long-term agenda for own area of responsibility;
- has a clear vision for the years ahead and aligns organizational resources to where the business, market, and function need to go;
- able to spot previously unidentified business opportunities; and
- implements successful business strategy that challenges the overall organization and other players in the industry.

Change Leadership

This leader carries integrated changes within a business to achieve a sustainable competitive advantage. The leader

- inspires and energizes others to embrace new ways of doing things;
- demonstrates a willingness to take appropriate risks and adopts an "out of the box" thinking;
- takes action to influence specific individuals, such as giving them a part to play in the change effort;
- engages others internally and externally by making the case for change and explaining their role in it;
- publicly tracks the progress of the change in order to keep people engaged; and
- engages with people throughout the change process to understand and address emotional reactions and maintain commitment.

Team Leadership

The team leader has the ability to empower, grow, develop, and inspire high-performing teams and individuals. He/she

- provides team with clear directions and makes link with organizational goals;
- provides clear objectives, a sense of team identity, and holds team accountable for meeting collective goals;
- demonstrates inspirational leadership and empowers the team to identify and solve problems, providing necessary support;
- recognizes,encourages, and rewards individual initiatives to advance the common goal;
- has a clear view of how the different capabilities of team members work together;
- acts as a role model of Teva's core values and code of conduct;
- takes responsibility for all people development processes and grow the next generation in line with business/unit needs;
- holds others accountable for their actions. Accepts accountability for own decisions and behaviors; and
- treats others with dignity and respect.

Professional Expertise

The individual demonstrates a particular and specific knowledge that significantly contributes to the company. This individual

- demonstrates in-depth knowledge of the profession and possesses wide experience and exposure to best practices;
- proactively mentors and shares his/her professional knowledge across the organization; and
- demonstrates deep understanding of solutions that could impact the other parts of the organization and sees applicability of current functional solutions to address current business issues.

Collaboration and Influencing

The leader in this category has the ability to influence in increasingly complex situations, to integrate diverse inputs and to develop effective working relationship to positively impact business performance. He/she recognizes and works across global line of differences,

- builds relationships, foregoing personal objectives for the benefit of the group;
- takes calculated and realistic steps to advance collaboration;
- uses the informal structure, organizational network, dynamics, and culture of the organization to get things done;
- brings people together across boundaries (global and local) to achieve results as a team and to share best practices;
- works very closely with key leaders across the business and in the external environment to ensure cross-fertilization;
- develops or supports actions consistent with global requirements while taking into account local needs; and
- demonstrates sensitivity and respect to employees and/or customers across geographic and cultural boundaries.

Business Acumen

An individual has the ability to scan widely, identify business opportunities, and apply business and industry knowledge and practices into integrated activities and processes. He/she understands what it takes to be a leading company,

- contributes value to organization through initiatives beyond own area;
- actively draws insight from a wide variety of internal and external sources, to generate new ideas and opportunities for his/her own and other parts of business;
- creates new business opportunities by building cross-functional company or industry partnerships; and
- understands market influence and competition and effectively uses that knowledge to create competitive advantage.

4

What and Where?

Commitment to Excellence

Accepting a status quo is accepting average and not seeking advancement to higher level, which is the biggest hindrance to higher achievement. However, gearing for results requires a leadership trait, well-established core competency, streamlined simple culture of discipline, emphasis on technologies, and a balanced recognition that radical change causes failures. Looking at company results alone is not enough. Circuit city was reported to achieve 18.5 times market returns between 1982 and 1997; nonetheless, they filed for bankruptcy later on. Fannie Mae was reported to achieve 7.5 times results for 15 years continuously. It fell apart following the major market fallout of 2008.

A well-defined strategy strikes a comparison between qualitative quick movers, and not against quantitative analyses. Executive and workers' compensation are kept at par. Bonuses are calculated based on relative individual and company overall performance. A balance is sought between grown management and fresh blood to infuse talent acquisition. The built theories are derived from the evidence. What is different? (a question at large.)

Grow management from within the core competencies. Limit executive compensation to delineate controversy. Select what to do. Select what not to do? Technologies must be carefully selected such that they will not derail transformation and advancement. Recognize that acquisition to create growth can be a double-edged sword. This usually involves managing people, creating change, creating alignment through commitment, motivation, and reward. Programs should not be highly publicized. They need to be merely happening as part of daily business. Leap results are not revolution in process.

Seeking excellence is by choice and by design. The goal is to organize information and bring order and clarity to processes to go from chaos to orderly execution. This requires leadership to emphasize on humility, empathy, and professional development. One needs to look at the vision with an unrelentless positive attitude and a deep desire to succeed. It is imperative to rotate people to gain broader sense of understanding of various functions of business operations without disrupting their career path. Indeed, encouragement is essential, but abilities in each different role have to be tested along the way. Broader understanding and leadership perspectives have to be built. A passion to be the best in field and working toward achieving that whether it is in product or service is critical to the pursuit of excellence. Consistent diligence and persistence requires tremendous discipline. Therefore, maintaining an open mind and having a free will while managing situations will help in achieving greater results and higher performance.

Nothing would seem like a miracle when the entrepreneurial spirit is on the rise. When there is planned action that is conceptually sound and based on thorough testing producing repeatable results, it will ensure great performance. Once the basics are built, one must continue to build on it and create a system that will ensure sustainable performance and delivery of desired results.

Sequentially, researching and collecting data, organizing data to understand trends, testing one's thesis through different variables, graphs, and plotting the data, correlating the data to physical observations, making rules based on these observations, and repeating all of these several times elevates one to a higher level of understanding. After these, conclusions should be drawn and further action should be taken accordingly. You need to make your move.

Human nature entice us with hope, yearning, love, hate, jealousy, envy, desire, eagerness, wants, etc. Link your human desires to your business problems. If your desires are average, normal, and complacent, then you will achieve that easily and it will be difficult to visualize the higher level. Only when you seek excellence, and are unrelenting, you move to the higher level. Never give up, be patient, and continue on the road with smartness and hard work, with definitive goals and a clear vision of your path ahead.

Leadership

Leaders are focused on accomplishments irrespective of who gets the credit. Sometimes you might come across a leader who appears to have an awkward shyness, but is genuine, with a fierce courage and resolve to attack and resolve issues in their lives.

It all starts by emphasizing talent and building knowledge, honing skills, and establishing discipline. A leader works within a team and effectively interacts with team members. A leader defines the specific goals and goes after them relentlessly and with an organized plan. He/she always raises the standards to achieve higher levels of performance through the pursuit of excellence. A refined leader will conduct himself/herself with utmost humility and will continuously build his/her professional competencies based on a wide-angle vision and bigger picture objectives. His/her positive and unwavering will to succeed will surely bring success to others. Trying to define leadership and placing it as the answer to everything is counterproductive.

Hence, leaders should focus on the quiet practice of leadership behavior encouraging their followers to approach their projects/tasks with vigor and excitement.

Effective leaders always figure things out in a simple and modest way and tend to accomplish what they set out to and envisioned. They easily convince their followers about what is ahead by clearly showing them the target and the path to reach it. Leaders are always willing to demonstrate and teach to help their followers know of what is desired.

Executives must make unselfish choices by forgoing certain amount of money for agreed compensation or bonuses to ensure that a sense of giving is established within an organization. This is specifically important when an organization is going through difficult times and is under public scrutiny. Charitable activities and community involvement are revelations to followers and reflective of the kindness, care, and empathy that the leader possesses. Leaders need to leave a positive impact and a real legacy so that they would be remembered favorably.

Leaders are excellent listeners, quiet, humble, modest, reserved, gracious, highly efficacious, understanding, and caring. They appear as very ordinary people, but with very high and extraordinary accomplishments. Leaders acknowledge credit to others as fairly as possible. When things go bad, they always bear the responsibility first.

A true leader is a truth seeker, who will use his will and powers to improve the situation as need be. Leaders need to produce successful and sustainable results that in turn would bring benefits and financial profits. Work hard, work hard, and work hard in smart strides.

Social Media

As technology evolved, the trend of social media has surpassed all odds by taking the market into avenues, starting with search engines such as Alta Vista, Yahoo, and Google, which developed more into social forums such as MySpace, Facebook, Twitter, and LinkedIn, which are leading cutting-edge communications platforms for social and professional contacts.

Recently, social media has been changing the face of brand promotions. Several companies are exploring websites such as Twitter, Facebook, LinkedIn, online forums, blogs, etc. to boost their marketing activities. Social media platforms are thus used to generate sales either inducing trial by giving coupons, free samples, etc., or by enhancing customer engagement. It also provides an open platform for customers to post and express their opinions and share their experiences.

As consumers are becoming more tech-savvy, social media platforms also provide an avenue to evaluate various options before the actual purchase, and thus aid in pre-purchase online research. In addition, social media has played a vital role in the emergence of new trends such as consumption of healthier and organic food items, specialty nutritional vitamins, and pharmaceutical health enhancement products, as consumers can discuss their choices and share their experiences. Apart from this, social media can also be used to gauge consumer perception and to provide active customer service by addressing customer questions, complaints, and inquiries.

Major players are fighting to maximize the number of fans on social media platforms such as Facebook, and have been spending around 15 percent of the total advertising budget on online models. Social media is certainly a growing future trend of brand promotions as companies are further exploring to discover new avenues.

Wireless Technologies

Wireless is the largest technology platform in history—it affects nearly every person and industry on every continent. Let us take, for example, Qualcomm's wireless solutions. Qualcomm® platform enables augmented reality (AR) applications to reach across most mobile environments. Qualcomm's Vuforia software platform uses computer vision-based image recognition giving developers the freedom to extend support for iOS, Android, and Unity 3D technologies. The Vuforia platform allows writing a single native application that can reach users across a wide range of smart phones and tablets. When it comes to context aware-ness, Gimbal™ for Android and iOS, from Qualcomm Labs, is designed to deliver timely, relevant, personalized content to mobile audiences where and when they need it most. Gimbal is equipped with intuitive tools, like image recognition and privacy controls.

Mobile technologies for automotives, transportation, and logistics are evolving to develop next-generation car telemetric applications. The same cellular communications technologies that are enabling billions of devices are now enabling utility companies to reliably and cost-effectively deploy smarter grids. Cellular modem solutions facilitate connectivity for consumer applications such as personal emergency response systems (PERS) and mobile health. Enabling "digital home environ-ments" means the home network in the future must have full home coverage, simplicity (no new wires), energy efficiency, scalability, interoperability, and security.

Peer-to-peer technology enables exciting new user experiences from multiplayer gaming and entertainment to media sharing, productivity tools, and social networking.

Development of 3G technologies is now driving America's larg-est-ever deployment of electric vehicles (EVs) and EV-charging infrastructure to enable integration with the country's emerging smart energy grid.

Industrial automation and enterprise offer cellular connectiv-ity and computing solutions that enable enterprises and retail segments such as ATMs, vending machines, and point-of-sale systems, which utilize 3G/4G modem solutions for reliable and fast connection with cellular networks. Connectivity is also complemented with Wi-Fi and home plug-in solutions.

Digital signage and remote displays can leverage the powerful processing and graphics capabilities of all-in-one mobile processors. Enterprise tracking applications benefit from cell tower positioning, Wi-Fi positioning, and various other techniques for precise asset and people location.

Wireless charging solutions for a complex, high-tech world such as mobile phones, tablets, portable electronics, power tools, EVs, all have something in common—currently all require cables or wires to charge up. Qualcomm has developed a pair of wireless charging solutions—one for portable electronics and another for EVs—designed to decrease the clutter caused by today's charging cables and wires, simplifying the charging of mobile devices, electronics, and EVs.

Forward Error Correction (FEC) technologies are designed to recover data missing for any reason, including network packet loss. This technology enhances file delivery and streaming solutions. For example, wireless service providers can offer high-quality mobile broadcast and streaming video services to customers; enterprises can broadcast time-sensitive database updates to remote sites; and military organizations can stream real-time surveillance video in harsh communications environments. Its flexible application programming interface (API) and high-performance decoding algorithm make it a versatile error-correcting code for all types of content delivery and streaming video services.

Earlier, graphics were practical only on desktop PCs, visually compelling mobile applications such as advanced user interfaces, Web browsers, navigation programs, and games, but nowadays, they are widely seen and used on mobile devices. To obtain optimal performance while minimizing battery drain, device manufacturers are relying on hardware graphics acceleration such as that delivered by integrated graphics solution. Graphics tools include powerful graphics content creation, profiling, analysis, and optimization.

Internet-connected devices such as smartphones, tablets, set-top boxes, and televisions are becoming more influential in the way people watch and share video content. As such, the state of video consumption is poised for explosive growth based simply on the different types of devices that can be found in connected homes.

The video processing engine is the part of a processor that is responsible for image quality. One of its many functions is to convert and format video data from any source and display it on the screen without loss of picture quality. It also takes incoming video streams at different resolutions and scales them to the proper one before displaying it on the screen. Many sources provide video in interlaced format that must be converted to a progressive format before it can be displayed, although how well these conversions are performed varies across different video processing engines. These engines can perform these conversions effortlessly and elegantly to produce the highest quality images displayed on the screen. In addition, many video sources are prone to visual noise that comes about as a result of poor capture, poor transmission, or overcompression. A video processing engine contains advanced algorithms for noise reduction as well as image formatting and conversion. It also contains image enhancement algorithms that add detail to low-resolution images and adjust color and contrast to give crisp, clear images on display.

Wireless Security

To deliver trusted services, the security suite is a key component of multimedia suite, providing operators, manufacturers, and wireless users confidence in the integrity and security of the wireless network and the wireless device. New, attractive services are enabled by maintaining the confidentiality and integrity of value-added services, in addition to providing protection for the distribution of premium digital media.

The digital rights management (DRM) platform enables new and compelling business models; a trust agent controls access to sensitive personal data for e-commerce services such as wallet, ticketing, and online payment, and other private information such as location determination. In addition, the trust agent enables the delivery of highly secure services, including strong identification and authentication capabilities, to deliver protected wireless networks for enterprises with mobile workers.

Connecting everything® isn't just Broadcom's tagline, it's a vision of the future—a world in which connectivity is at the heart of interactions with technology and with each other. Broadcom's broadband connectivity chips enable high-speed delivery of secure Internet access, IP-based voice service, video teleconferencing, and hundreds of digital and high-definition television channels to homes and small businesses over wired and wireless networks. Broadcom's broadband solutions are designed for cable, DSL, PON, satellite, and hybrid IP equipment, including cable modem, cable set-top box, digital transport adapters, and high-definition audio / video / graphics system processors. Wireless networking technology extends the reach of shared broadband Internet access, video transfer, and voice at high speeds to homes and businesses through wireless networks. Chips and software are incorporated into cellular handsets, wireless LANs, and Bluetooth™ personal area network (PAN) products.

Network Infrastructure

Design and development of complete silicon and software solutions for service providers, data centers, enterprises, and small-to-medium business networks involve solutions that leverage industry-proven Ethernet technology to promote faster, greener, and more cost-efficient transport and processing of voice, video, and data across both wired and wireless networks. The use of 2G, 3G, and 4G baseband processors, cellular RF, mobile multimedia processors, mobile TV receivers, power management solutions, and GPS are specific examples that facilitate these objectives. These technologies enable a network infrastructure that is scalable, secure, and easy to manage. These products are found in a wide variety of networking equipment including Ethernet switches, routers and gateways, security appliances, 3G/4G wireless backhaul equipment, cable and VoIP hardware, desktop and notebook computers, servers and storage appliances, and network-attached printers.

Advances in Radio

Radio networks such as PodcastOne.com is a one-stop site that offers shows from hundreds of online broadcasters for listeners to browse and download. Podcasts are shows available online, which listeners can hear on their computers or download onto their smartphones, iPods, tablets, or other devices. Unlike conventional radio, a podcast can be saved, stopped, replayed, and consumed at the listener's leisure. Podcasts give the opportunity to put out content to a mass audience without the constraint of approval from a program director or a station group. Many of the programs are archived versions of a host's radio shows or extra content beyond those programs. Podcasts may be attractive to advertisers, similar to radio, but different in measures. Traditionally, radio advertisements are sold based on the number of estimated listeners. With Podcasts, the basis is the number of downloads, which is a fixed number compared to an estimate.

E-Commerce

Similar to Amazon.com, overstock.com, Groupon Inc. is one of the largest daily-deal website that markets and sells on the Internet, but promotes the use of discount coupons. One question that remains for Groupon business model is its increased reliance on Groupon physical goods, since selling physical products is less profitable than service-type typical spa and restaurant vouchers. While boosting Groupon overall inventory of deals is probably helpful, it would be a bad sign if its reliance on low-margin product deals keeps rising, which in turn will affect its stock price and market value.

Entrepreneurship

Innovative entrepreneurs practice discovery-driven leadership, according to Hal Gregersen, professor of innovation and leadership at Insead School of business in France. By contrast, the defining traits of conventional delivery-driven leadership include analyzing, planning, detail orientation, and self-discipline. The entrepreneur's change agents typically embody the following ingredients:

- Unconventional associations: drawing connections between questions, problems, or ideas in unrelated fields.
- Uncommon questioning: posing queries that challenge common wisdom.
- Diversified networking: meeting people with different ideas and perspectives.
- Creative observing: scrutinizing the behavior of customers, suppliers, and competitors to identify new ways of doing things.
- Unorthodox experimenting: constructing interactive experiences and providing innovative responses to see what insights emerge.
- Developing a mindset that is self-reinforcing, optimisms that would scale up little sparks to create a continuum that is integrated

and in some way meaningful, irrespective of key policy or regulatory issues.

• Developing an attitude with excitement to continuously pursue the discovery of the unknown and look forward to be part of the next big thing that will impact humanity. Utilize education, empirical knowledge, learning experiences, and daily activities with utmost curiosity to innovate and create.

5

Facts and Faith?

Systematically, leaders in an organization need to develop meaningful metrics to assess profit per base unit (profit per employee, profit per customer visit, etc.) Examples of denominators could be per employee, geographical region, risk level; per customer; per brand; per quantity of finished goods; per group of people, etc. The value of these metrics is in measuring the performance of a company over a period of time to observe trends and try to separate events from established processes that affect the company's overall performance and profitability over time. These metrics should be based on scientific principles to ensure that the measurements reflect realities that stand behind the health and longevity of the organization. This chapter highlights the key interests that a scientific approach and methodology will preserve to ensure that company procedures follow acceptable principles that will lead to success.

The Scientific Method

The basis for all thinking behind the difference between facts and faith is the scientific method. Steps of the scientific method include:

- *Asking a question*
- *Doing background research*

- *Constructing a hypothesis*
- *Testing the hypothesis by doing an experiment*
- *Analyzing the data and drawing a conclusion*
- *Communicating the results*

The scientific method is a systematic sequence of techniques for investigating phenomena based on observations and experimentation. To be termed scientific, a method of inquiry must be based on experience and measurable evidence subject to specific principles of reasoning that are related to natural laws of physics and verified through mathematical calculations. The *Oxford English Dictionary* says that the scientific method is "a method or procedure that has characterized natural science since the 17th century, consisting in systematic observation, measurement, and experiment, and the formulation, testing, and modification of hypotheses."

The chief characteristic that distinguishes the scientific method from other methods of acquiring knowledge is that scientists seek objective reality, supporting a theory when a theory's predictions are confirmed through physical testing, and challenging a theory when its predictions prove false. Scientific researchers propose hypotheses as explanations of phenomena, and design experimental studies to test these hypotheses via predictions that can be derived from them. These steps must be repeatable, to guard against mistake or confusion in any particular experimentation. Scientific inquiry is generally intended to be as objective as possible in order to reduce biased interpretations of results, which must be correlated statistically for significance of occurrence. Another basic expectation is to document, archive, and share all data and methodology so that they are available for careful scrutiny by other scientists and investigators (peer reviewed), giving them the opportunity to verify results by attempting to reproduce them. This practice of full disclosure also allows statistical measures for the reliability of these data to be established and provides for mathematical models for prediction of similar results.

Measuring Economic Profit

Now that we established acceptable methodology for seeking facts that will help businesses select the right approaches for measurement, one major requirement is to be able to predict and calculate economic value for an organization. Economic profit is equal to the percent return on investment less than the percent cost of capital as a function of the invested capital. In other words, the economic profit is the ratio of earnings to invested capital. Since earnings are equivalent to revenue less personnel cost less supplier costs less depreciation, then, factor in the number of people employed and use two metrics, employee productivity and average personnel cost per person employed, which implies: economic profit is equal to employee productivity less average cost for people employed.

Who? Then How, What, and When

When we look at a person, we usually like the ones who are similar to us. Nonetheless, keep an open mind for differences in styles of leadership. Many a time, people will surprise us by doing things differently. Basic traits might be similar, but the approach, speed order, and other factors might be placed differently that would bring an equally important result, even if it is performed and approached differently.

Besides measurement, selecting the right talent is crucial to an organization's future growth. It is imperative to start the reaction and look for results. Look for self-motivated people, intelligent, innovative, and creative, and they will devise the best goals for the future of the organization based on a simple strategy. They will refine strategy to accomplish higher levels. Leaders should make sure that both the organization as well as the employees are mutually benefited. It is a two-way street. If you are searching for excellence and you are in a mediocre environment that does not fit your nature, make a move and continue searching for what you believe is your right fit and right environment. Only then, you will excel and get motivated to achieve higher goals.

The motivation to be able to successfully continue the quest for excellence is complex. Compensation will serve up to a certain motivation level. Beyond that, the right factors must be in place to usher higher performance levels. The right people will do the right things and deliver irrespective of the compensation and rewards. It should be there, but it is not, ultimately, the only thing that makes leaders move forward. The right people, the right compensation, the right behaviors, and then the right results, will lead to excellence. Consistently, hiring the right people, extracting efficient work from them, and paying them well are expected measures to support in building the road to excellence. Hardworking people will thrive, and lazy people will snap and leave. The right people possess character, educational standards, practical approach, skilled knowledge, and specific experiences. It is important to lead, and not mislead, people. To let people go on with uncertainty is a selfish undertaking that is ill-received. Rather, people need to know where they stand such that they can go on with their lives. Leaders need to argue and debate vigorously to seek the best possible pathway. Nevertheless, they need to unite behind a decision regardless of interests. Leaders enjoy their time in conducting their effort as if it is a personal affair. They build brotherhoods, friendships that will last a lifetime, or for decades, to come remain close to those in their path, even if they leave their company.

Look for facts and do not cling to false hopes. Confront the brutal facts (Collins, 2001). Results are due to the concentrated effort of organizing activities and data with clear objectives. Sound decisions have to be diligently executed to achieve desirable results. It is significant to pay attention to data and focus on the facts of the matter. As we look for the truth, many things come in our way that would be revolting and detrimental. It is necessary to remain focused on the effort to achieve an ultimate outcome. We must build a culture that is very hostile to complacency. No matter how good the result is, it should be perceived as a steppingstone to a better condition. It should never be enough, and thus will sustain great results.

Charisma can be as much of a liability as an asset. People might just tell you what they think you like to hear. Along the way, one must continue looking for the facts. Also, continue to motivate people, but watch out for false hopes, as they are detrimental. The desired leadership environment is where truth is always welcome, even if it means having to confront the brutal facts (Collins, 2001). Truth can be revealed best using the question and answer method. This approach ensures a deeper understanding of the issues at hand. With humility, questions should be very selective to unravel the truth. Questions must lead to the best possible insight on the subject that needs to be uncovered. Developing dialogue and debate, rather than pushing through opinions are key approaches to moving forward with the issues at hand. Investigative measures also often reveal the truth. Threatening, instead of training and encouragement, will not bring about improvement. Developing information for the sake of information is counterproductive. Information should be used effectively to enhance current situations and conditions.

Always listen to the voice of the customers. Ensure that they have the upper hand in deciding what their expected outcome is. Making sure they only support or pay only what they believe to be fair is the only prediction for future potential orders. One must retain habitual/regular and repeat customers to ensure a sustainable business. Listing the facts and letting the customer decide is a more sustainable business conduct for repeat selling. Overpowering the customer with charisma is not long-lasting. Rather, approach the customer with ultimate humility.

Displaying patience in the face of calamity is a major characteristic of leadership. One must never give up and always think of the positive outcome that will prevail. It would be a turnaround experience in any case. Collins has repeatedly asserted, "Confront the brutal facts." Deal with the difficult issues. Plan and execute to mitigate the effects of detriments. When it is surmounting events, quiet the mind, and proceed with calmness. Maintain faith that you will prevail regardless of how difficult the situation. Moving forward and confronting what is ahead will help one focus and prevent divergence in the face of difficulties.

Taking a complex world and simplifying it is a safe approach to winning (e.g., Einstein and "relativity," Adam Smith and "division of labor," Karl Marx and "workers of the world unite." Focusing on what one is passionate about in one's core competency spearheads and paves the road to accomplishment. One must lead to be the best with respect to what one is passionate about, and also be able to manage the financial plan. Significantly, understanding the situation and managing according to abilities rather than showing pride will be well received. Attempting to do what one can is more realistic. It is essential to apply the fundamental principles of leadership constantly, else there can be a roll back.

A culture of discipline will focus on competence, and placing the right people in the right place will increase effectiveness and eliminate bureaucracy. The goal is to create a balance to motivate people while reducing hierarchy. It is important to create consistent symmetry across the organization. Promoting entrepreneurship, but ensuring discipline is essential as well. For example, as plans can change, adjusting and readjusting to focus on obtaining meaningful results is also important. No matter how tough the measure, focusing on what you have accomplished relative to what you have stated to have accomplished is the right measure, that is, balancing accountability with responsibility. Maintaining rigor and discipline to enable creativity, innovation, and entrepreneurship should be one of the main goals of motivating team members in an organization. Disciplined action should be the result of disciplined people and their ideas, not the opposite: Rigorous planning, market analysis, operations research and analysis, profit analysis, cost controls, and benchmarking are examples of key operating parameters that will guide one through to success. The challenge is not in opportunity creation or finding, but in opportunity selection and choice. Opportunity must fit the company profile, core competency, the best in class ranking and, above all, make sense economically. Drawing a balance between management and worker interests is important. Budgeting should follow the discipline to decide where to spend. Activities that support the company's world-class objectives should be considered first.

This work's focus is on how leaders can survive and succeed in organizations by evolving the organizational culture and the capability and commitment of employees. It provides and illustrates powerful and yet conceptually simple messages, for example, the need for simplicity of communication, the need to ensure problem-solving teams to have diverse and challenging constituents, and the importance of having a bias to action. The message's strength is that in adopting the tenet of the importance of human nature, it effectively bridges the gap between other texts' reliance on deep theories of organizational psychology (e.g., Elliott Jaques's defining work *Requisite Organization: Total System for Effective Managerial Organization and Managerial Leadership for the 21st Century*) and commentators relying primarily on their experiences of management. We view leaders as shaping the generally natural selection–based evolution of an organization's culture and mode of work. Therefore, the sequence of positioning the importance of leadership and its practice in the vanguard, followed by the selection, development, and motivation of people, and then the importance of enablers such as innovation, technology, and maintaining broad direction and simplicity of thinking are clear indications on the importance of effective allocation of accountability in assigning tasks and roles to individuals and teams, and providing guidance on how this should be done to ensure that expectations are mutually understood. Failures in this area are all too common and a measure of formality may be required before it becomes second nature. One must resist any urge to overweigh the role of technology in what this message is fundamentally about—the shaping and role of human nature in organizations.

Elliott Jaques developed the notion of requisite organization, which is a unified whole system model for effective managerial leadership. He developed the concept of "social systems as defense against unconscious anxiety" (Jaques, 1997), which sheds light on the close relationship between organizational task (i.e., the main aim of an organization, such as to produce, cure, etc.) and unconscious group dynamics and how each can aid or distort the other. He is most widely known for his concept of the "time-span of discretion," a measure of how much responsibility an employee has. Jaques argued that the higher a person was in a hierarchy, the longer he could work to complete a task without supervision. The time span of a CEO of a major institution might be 15–20 years. This concept enabled him to describe a "requisite organization" as one in which each level in the hierarchy had its own distinctive time span. If an organization had too many levels, then their time spans overlapped. In this case, managers at a higher level would interfere in the work of managers at a lower level. The process of delegation would be undermined leading to preposterous organizational dysfunction. This is consistent with the horizontal organizational structure that demands flattening of the organization for improved effectiveness. The following points highlight some key elements of the requisite organization theory of organizational development (OD):

- Nearly all organizational dysfunction can be traced to poor structure and systems, not deficient employees.
- OD interventions should focus upon fixing the organization rather than fixing employees. Fixing the organization (e.g., structure, role relationships, policies, systems of work, managerial practices) frees employees to work at their full potential creating increased efficiency, effectiveness, and employee satisfaction.
- Examples of fixing the organization include science-based methodologies for:
  1. matching employee capability to job complexity;
  2. appropriately spacing employees' capability with that of their managers to improve leadership and communication;
  3. ensuring the right number of organizational layers;
  4. explicitly defining managerial authority and accountability;
  5. explicitly defining managerial leadership processes;
  6. explicitly defining cross-functional working relationships; and
  7. matching compensation to job complexity (felt fair compensation).

Many thought patterns and motivators, which are reflective of the spiritual nature of man that explain the reference of many spiritual beliefs across the globe are dependent on four pillars of human thought—namely, physical nature, rational methods of reasoning, emotional connections, and spiritual drives. The main values in the pursuit of drivers for survival to growth in one's journey are consistent with the strive to establish balance among these pillars of thought patterns in this paradigm that is behind successes and failures in people's careers.

6

Discipline and Goal Setting

Disciplined people do not need hierarchy. Disciplined thoughts do not need bureaucracy. Disciplined action and ethical entrepreneurship create great performance. Many leading global companies started with ambitions that were far bigger than their resources and capabilities. Nevertheless, they had an obsession for winning at all levels of the organization and sustained that obsession for decades. Table 6.1 reports on key factors by raising the bar annually.

Setting Goals

Many firmly believe that setting goals is extremely important to stay focused and motivated, which ultimately leads to

Table 6.1 Vital Factors to Enhance Performance

You	Present	1 year later (10%)
Planning	1.00	1.10
Organizing	1.00	1.10
Staffing	1.00	1.10
Leading	1.00	1.10
Communicating	1.00	1.10
Deciding	1.00	1.10
Controlling	1.00	1.10
Output	7.00	7.70

accomplishments, growth, and satisfaction. You can achieve anything with clear goals—anything! Ten good reasons to set goals are:

1. They force you to define your value system.
2. They force you to set priorities.
3. They identify a track for you to follow.
4. They help you manage your behavior.
5. They help you identify your strength and weaknesses.
6. They improve your self-esteem.
7. They get you to focus your energy.
8. They motivate you.
9. They make you stretch.
10. They will make you a winner.

"Whatever the mind can conceive and believe, it can achieve" (Napoleon Hill, Think and Grow Rich.)

In today's hypercompetitive market, creating new advantages faster and on time is one of the key factors for a company's success. This is especially true for R&D–based companies where making or breaking development schedules could translate into success or failure, respectively.

Based on the above facts, it is important to identify the organizational behaviors and elements that may affect the development cycles in R&D–based companies in order to apply the necessary paradigms to achieve the desired performance levels.

The following scenario describes an analysis on a software R&D company's effort to assist the company's senior management in determining as to why project deadlines were not met despite the management's exhaustive attempts to motivate the employees in achieving the preset project completion dates.

In order to understand the organizational deficiencies that contribute to this problem, numerous interviews were conducted with both the management and the staff. This complex problem of not meeting development cycle deadlines was attributed by

some managers as being the result of employees' lack of performance. The staff, on the other hand, identified the problem as the
use of high-pressure tactics by management to attain results.

Overall, ineffective communications, absent employee
involvement, lack of organizational structure, and inadequate
feedback process create the need to improve performance in this
company. After analyzing all the relevant facts, the underlying
problem appeared to be lack of goal setting.

A simple concept such as goal setting can direct attention,
mobilize effort, create persistence, and lead to strategy development to achieve goals, which in turn will improve the performance of the employees in meeting project deadlines (Locke,
1993). Furthermore, it was found that employees lacked motivation and commitment to goals simply because there were no
clearly set goals. Finally, the process of setting and complying
with R&D schedules is a complex and multidimensional task
that requires preplanning and clear foresight. Therefore, it is
not the intention to imply that goal setting is the panacea to the
stated problem; nonetheless, goal setting is a practical managerial tool that has shown to be a highly effective technique
in managing performance with no direct financial cost to the
company (Sims and Lorenzi).

Goal theory is widely attributed to Edwin A. Locke. Goals
are conscious cognitive regulators of behavior. Goals are part
of a broad category of antecedents that precede behavior. First,
a goal must be set and then appropriate behaviors can follow.
It is unrealistic to expect goal-directed behaviors without first
setting goals. Examples of goals are deadlines, budgets, and
quotas, just to name a few. It is sometimes quoted that goals are
dreams with deadlines. Goals keep us focused on what needs to
be accomplished.

For a goal to be most effective, attention must be directed to
the characteristics of the goal or goal attributes. These attributes

concern the choice of goals, the process of setting goals, and the ongoing pursuit of the goal once it is set. According to Sims and Lorenzi, these five attributes are: goal specificity, goal difficulty, feedback, participation in goal setting, and competition in the goal achievement process. Specific goals are better than ambiguous goals because results can be measured and action plans to meet the goals can be drafted.

Difficult yet attainable goals lead to higher performance. The reason difficult goals lead to higher performance is related to the increased challenge of the task. However, if goal difficulty becomes too great, an employee might feel that the goal is unachievable and give up. The purpose is on increasing performance and not completely on goal attainment. Feedback between the manager and the employee is essential in the goal-setting process. Feedback can be categorized into two types: process feedback and discrepancy feedback. Process feedback is provided to the employee as the attainment of the goal is being sought. This type of feedback should provide the employee information as to how effective his/her efforts are in achieving the goal. Discrepancy feedback is provided once the tasks of goal attainment are completed and show how closely the results match with the goal. Participative goal setting is one that involves employees in the goal-setting process with the management. This includes determining what the goals are going to be and the associated goal difficulty timetable. Competition in goal attainment can occur in many forms. Employees can either compete with the goal directly, with the performance of members of the group, or with historical achievements of the group. Competition can increase the specificity and the difficulty of the goal. Dysfunctional competition can occur if the competition is between interdependent groups or employees. Before goals can lead to higher performance, the employee must first accept them. Goals that are perceived by the employee as fair and reasonable are more likely to be accepted. Additionally, the employee should view these goals as beneficial. The employee must feel that the goals are in his/her own best interest, and not just in the best interest of management. Using goals as a clarifying device will also aid in employee goal acceptance. Goal commitment is essential to goal attainment as it is imperative that employees continually endeavor toward goal attainment even in times of difficulty. Contingent incentives, which are delivered only upon the successful attainment of the goal, such as monetary rewards, time off, promotions, managerial praise, and recognition can be used in combination with goal attributes to ensure goal commitment. Once the goal participant has accepted and committed to the goals, the participant should be provided ample means for attaining the desired goal achievement level. This requires that the management provides adequate resources such as manpower, vendors, tools, and computers, freedom to use these tools, and managerial help. Goal participants must feel that they can come to the management at any time, for any reason, and that the management will support them with whatever is needed to achieve the goals.

"Standardize on goal setting as part of your organizational culture"—by this, we mean make goal setting a regular way of managing projects. Continuously provide training to support new methods of goal setting and also reinforce the current methods. Once the company has a work group full of competent and highly efficacious employees, it can then focus on goal setting. Mentoring can be a superior technique in the development of self-efficacy. Mentoring provides an opportunity to increase employee self-efficacy through vicarious learning and verbal persuasion. In the vicarious learning approach, the project management skills that need to be developed are identified. Employees then spend time observing their mentors performing the desired tasks with specific talents. After observing their mentor, employees are given the opportunity to rehearse their skills. Mentors should have the employees practice their skills until the desired job function can be performed proficiently and spontaneously (Bandura, 1997). While using this strategy, mentors should continually remind employees that it is possible to develop strong project management skills. The stronger an employee's conviction that skills can be acquired, the easier it will be to acquire the necessary project management abilities. Employees who tend to believe skills and ability are inherent have a more difficult time picking up new talents through vicarious learning.

Verbal persuasion provides another opportunity for mentors to develop employees. For example, when facing a complex task a mentor can sit down with the employee who is about to undertake the task and assure the worker that he/she has what it takes to complete the task. This type of support boosts self-efficacy by helping the employee believe that she/he has the personal ability to complete the task. When the employee encounters difficulty in the performance of the task, the mentor can demonstrate the proper way to overcome the obstacle and reassure the worker that he/she is capable of overcoming the current situation and completing the task. When using verbal persuasion, it is imperative that the employee's mentor be a respected individual in the firm with a proven record of accomplishment in complex projects. These characteristics give the mentor credibility in the eyes of the worker being coached.

Opportunity is another way to build employee self-confidence. Giving employees the opportunity to manage complex projects builds self-efficacy by providing workers with a point of reference. When managing a project of similar complexity in the future, employees can refer back to similar projects that where successfully completed and feel efficacious in their ability to manage the project. By giving employees the opportunity to manage progressively complex tasks, the organization ultimately builds a pool of project managers that can successfully oversee tasks of varying degrees of complexity. This technique works very well when combined with mentoring. Using verbal persuasion and modeling, the mentor can "coach" the project manager through the project up to the point of completion. Thus, the project manager learns key skills through vicarious learning and develops his/her confidence by receiving verbal persuasion and successfully completing a project. The next time the employee encounters a project of similar complexity, he/she can undertake it with the knowledge that he/she has successfully completed similar projects in the past.

Feedback is very important with regard to goal setting and project performance. Feedback is particularly relevant if the organization is encouraging self-set goals. If employees are allowed to set goals and determine the strategy to achieve those goals, then feedback should be administered by someone other than the employees setting the goals and the strategy. Mentors provide a very good avenue for providing external feedback. The feedback will allow employees to keep abreast of where they stand in relation to the project goals and take the appropriate action to either keep the project ahead of schedule or make up for lost ground. Once the project is complete, the mentor can provide outcome feedback to inform project managers of how they did in relation to milestones, goals, due dates, and project quality. This information will allow project managers to replicate successful activities or modify unsuccessful strategies / courses of action.

When building employee self-efficacy, management should ensure that the work environment is supportive and free from distractions. This is because situations such as stress, fear, and anxiety can impede the development of self-efficacy. Self-imposed goals give employees a feeling of control over their environment.

By setting their own project completion dates employees feel that the goals are within the limits of their own ability. This is not to say the goals set by management are beyond the employees' ability but rather, employees that set project completion date feel as though they are driving the project's requirements.

7

Growth: Sustainable, Repeatable, Fast, and Well Trained

Human Factors

Overall, self-efficacy positively influences work-related performance. The awareness is that the relationship between self-efficacy and work-related performance was moderated by task complexity. The identification of task complexity relates to organizational settings because it appears that task complexity and situational factors present in the work environment tend to weaken the relationship between self-efficacy and performance.

Specific suggestions based on practical implications are for managers to provide accurate description of tasks that employees are asked to perform. Unless the definitions of the task circumstances and attributes are provided in a clear and concise manner, employees may not be able to accurately assess the scope of complexity of the task and the required demands to perform it. This means that the employee may not fully know what they have to do, and thus will lack information for regulating their effort. As a result, this may lead to a faulty assessment of their perceived efficacy.

Complex tasks usually involve several possible paths for their execution, and the appropriate selection of specific technological means or resources are necessary for successful performance. Otherwise, even when the strongest employee believes that he / she can execute the means (technical execution), it may not lead to the successful performance outcome, which in turn can result in unjustifiable lowered self-efficacy.

Due to the greater cognitive and behavioral demands imposed by complex tasks, employees may not perceive enough personal capability to successfully perform complex undertakings. This is not about training; rather it is about enhancing the beliefs of employees that they can utilize their already-acquired skills to tackle complexities of this level.

Managers may have to provide additional training for developing effective behavioral and cognitive strategies for coping with complex tasks. Employees need to gauge the task to establish the conception of ability. Otherwise, any mistake perceived as a basis for incapability might imply lack of control, which lessens beliefs of self-efficacy for subsequent performance. If efficacy-enhancement programs are to be implemented, their timing should be close to the task employees are asked to perform. Employees should have clear and objective standards to gauge the level of complexity of the task and thereby performance accomplishment.

Task complexity is relevant in self-efficacy. Bandura et al. (1992) and other researchers pointed out that in addition to the regulative potential of self-efficacy for successful performance, the relative contribution of task complexity must be considered. Conceptually, task complexity represents multifaceted aspects with different challenging implications for the task performer.

Self-efficacy and leadership are major influencing concepts and key to patterns of thought and behavior that are of fundamental value to job-related performance in organizational settings. Self-efficacy is subjective and personal to an employee's beliefs in his own ability to organize and execute courses of action required to attain a designed performance level. It is the ability to perform a specific task suggesting a strong sense of potential to accomplish the task.

Self-efficacy is objectively correlated to task-related ability. The greater an individual's task ability, the higher the belief in self-efficacy. Furthermore, increase in self-efficacy is likely to lead to further increase in ability. If a person feels competent at a particular task, that would be a measure of self-efficacy. To quantify self-efficacy, we must be able to measure or classify its characteristics. The categorized elements of self-efficacy are:

1. magnitude of self-efficacy (the level of task difficulty or complexity within the same domain of performance);
2. generality of self-efficacy, which implies an employee's adaptability to a variety of similar task situations; and
3. strength of self-efficacy, as a measure of the degree of persistence and diligence reflecting the employee's resilience and sustainability belief.

Strengthening an employee's belief in his/her sense of effectiveness through empowerment (form of delegation) would strengthen his self-efficacy belief. The desire to master a task (mastery) to become a superior performer is related to the employee's self-efficacy, which causes him to persevere in completing the task. The probability of success on a specific task would increase, as the expectations are higher based on stronger self-efficacy beliefs. Employee self-efficacy is developed and managed through successful performance (mastery experience), vicarious experience (modeling: live and symbolic), verbal and social persuasion (including coaching and suggestion), and emotional arousal (attribution, relaxation, and feedback). Each of these factors is an influence on self-efficacy perceptions.

Self-efficacy enhances performance more than skill development (training). Individuals with the same skill level may have to perform at different levels and self-efficacy may emerge to be an important factor in explaining any differences. Bandura and Cervone (1986) found that self-efficacy and self-set goals were motivating even in the face of feedback that indicated earlier failure.

Effects of Self-efficacy on Occupational Stress

Workplaces are often structured in ways that breed conflict and create impediments to fulfilling role demands within available resources. Perceived self-efficacy to fulfill occupational demands also affects level of stress and the physical health of employees. Certain organizational conditions can undermine employees' beliefs in their occupational capabilities and exacerbate the adverse effects of low sense of coping efficacy. These include unrealistic workloads, technical demands, poor prospects for advancement, and lack of balance between work life and home life, among other unsatisfying factors.

With the invasion of information technology, computers, and electronic monitors and devices, major stress reducers such as perceived control and social support are being eliminated from the workplace, creating a stressful environment that saps satisfaction.

Increased competition in the global market demands shorter development and manufacturing cycle times, which means tighter control over work schedules and work productivity. In recent years, downsizing and reorganization created job layoffs and their derivative job insecurities. Major mergers and acquisitions created consolidation. To get rid of duplication, and to increase efficiency and shareholders' profits, many people werelaid off. All this presented major stressors at all organizational levels.

Human stress has been viewed mainly in terms of task demands that exceed an individual's perceived capability. This would be the most common source of emotional strain. In addition, stress arises when people are trapped in jobs below their capability. Stress can be produced by self-devaluation for not making better use of one's achieved levels of skill and talent, and by social stigmatization upon being passed over for promotion. Within the interactional model, efficacy beliefs affect appraisal and impact of organizational stressors affect physical health and emotional life of employees.

What is experienced as an occupational stressor depends on the level of perceived self-efficacy. Employees who have a low sense of self-efficacy are stressed by heavy work demands and role responsibilities. Those who have a high sense of efficacy might be frustrated and stressed by limited opportunities to make full use of their talent. There is evidence to suggest that beliefs in individual and collective efficacy may contribute to different forms of occupational stress arising from organizational constraints, role ambiguity, and workloads. A low sense of personal efficacy to fulfill job demands arouses anxiety that contributes to job dissatisfaction.

The chronic stressors in emotionally taxing occupations can give rise to the syndrome of reactions described as "burnout." The emotional exhaustion and lack of any sense of personal accomplishment can occur in any occupation where people face unceasing workloads and view what they are doing as neither much valued nor as providing a meaningful contribution. Moreover, these occupational difficulties tend to carry over into personal life (substance abuse, health problems, and marital discord).

People resort to behavioral or cognitive efforts to manage or cope with stressors. Employees may try to restructure their work situations and increase their knowledge and skills to lessen their distress. Perceived self-efficacy is one factor that predicts the form of adapting to emotionally taxing work. Those who have a high sense of efficacy resort to problem solving aids designed to improve their work situation. In contrast, those who believe there is little they can do to change the stressful aspects of their job resort to dysfunctional ways to cope with and to get relief from stress.

Some strategies for relieving stress rely on cognitive reappraisals of situations to make them less aversive. These include viewing problems as challenges and incentives to improve one's skills, focusing on positive aspects in otherwise negative situations by reexamining priorities and seeking solace from others. A low sense of efficacy fosters escapist coping (resort to drinking, drug use, overeating, and withdrawal of involvement in the work life), which is apt to make work life even worse. This is exacerbated through higher levels of emotional exhaustion and feelings of futility concerning personal accomplishments.

Prevention and reduction of occupational stress at the personal level requires employees to develop skills and self-efficacy needed to manage their work life in ways that provide them with a sense of accomplishment and pride in their work. At the organizational level, efforts to reduce vulnerability to occupational stress and burnout should also address the various ways in which employees' self-efficacy is undermined by the institutional practice. Employees need some control over matters that affect their work life and give them a sense of ownership for what they produce. Accountability for results that they control, upgrading their skill, and helpful feedback that enables them to achieve a greater sense of efficacy lead to successful and a less-stressful environment.

Materials Factors

Materials Requirements Planning (MRP)

To control material flows from various suppliers, assembly and manufacture in subsequent locations, and distribution across the supply chain to myriad customers involves complex planning and logistics. Companies resort to information technology that hands out computerized packages to provide for all the planning activities and all materials-related services such as purchasing transactions, bills of materials, bills of lading, invoicing, and bills of sale. All these complex relationships for advanced financial transactions require the development of materials (and manufacturing) requirement planning (MRP) systems. MRP is defined as a system that consists of a set of logically related procedures, decision rules, and records designated to translate a master production schedule into time-phased net requirements.

The human elements behind these systems are typically driven by departmental or business discipline with differing motivations. Nonetheless, a computerized tool is strategic for survival as it cuts through business disciplines such that no specific one is rewarded for integrating the output of these disciplines. It resolves the issues in which people who were willing to deal with ambiguity and responsibility had the best chance to succeed.

Computerized Manufacturing & Services

Computer-based automation for improved operational efficiency is constantly evolving. Most elements of this trend fall under the umbrella of manufacturing execution systems (MES), a term coined for computer-based controls, signal processing, and connection to the enterprise resource planning (ERP), over the entire planning / scheduling / production process. The goal of MES is to provide a layer of information management that exists between basic planning systems and corporate manufacturing control systems. Information relates to real-time data about quality, cost, and inventory. Control means making the systems run in a smooth, coordinated, and relatively error-free manner. This trend is still evolving as subject matter experts (SMEs) and

business leaders wrestle with how far to go with MES to include
business intelligence, data mining, and analytics.

The sophistication of these systems increases almost in
a relatively short time period, while the cost for this performance continues to vary inconsistently, which makes decisions
on implementation harder to make. Add to this the increasing cost of labor, materials, and capital, and the evaluation of
applications more complex. The technology bottlenecks are in
the vision systems and sensors. While processing equipment,
conveyers, software, microprocessors, and computers have pro-
gressed to a point where total automation is possible, these systems need accurate information about everything from color,
to texture, to consistency to do an accurate reporting. That is
where sensory controls come into play with the most difficult of
materials to read such as suspensions, emulsions, and thexotro-
pic materials. Computer-integrated manufacturing approach is
only as good as the sensor data that drive it. These challenges
can be exacerbated where paralysis by analysis, or information
overload, turns managers into data processors, who compare
only marginal productivity gains with the value of investment.

While few debate the necessity of some type of MES in the
modern processing operation, disagreements surface over the
degree to which it should be implemented. Strong advocates of
MES insist that complete implementation is necessary to fully
link plant floor data with administrative systems, while others,
who are less enthusiastic, see pitfalls in all-encompassing systems. More sophisticated automation has actually created dis-
ruptions in many cases. A lot of the closed loop controls might be
reacting to statistically insignificant variations, making adjust-
ments, including causing problems down-line and down-time
by super optimizing locally, compromising the overall system
and rendering it sub-optimal. Focusing on significant variables that really do need attention can minimize unnecessary

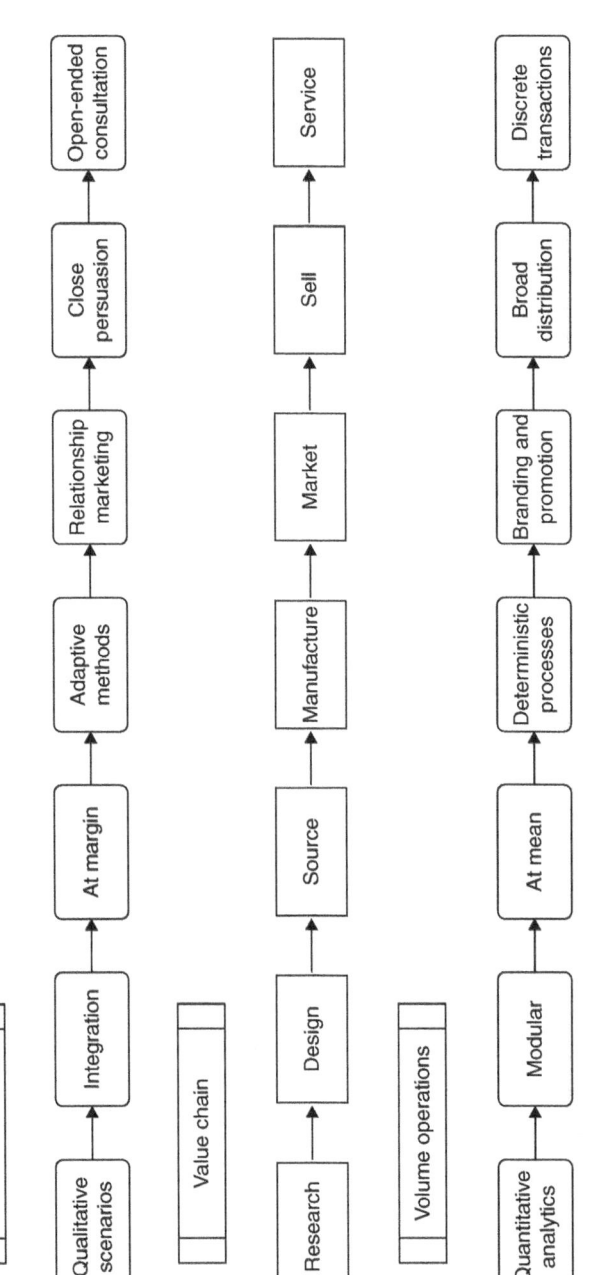

Figure 7.1 Value Chain Differences between Complex Systems and Volume Operations.

reactions, as against random variations and data. Data must be targeted based on the top three or four significant and statistically measured variables.

One major example is that you might spend all the money and time to design the software, train people, and still it might be one phone call from a person on the shop floor end saying that the line is down. A selection of applications for a continuous or batch process might govern the level of sophistication that could hamper more than it could help. Computerized automation, for example, in the area of continuous processing of raw ingredients, might improve quality and reduce waste.

Figure 7.1 highlights typical processes in the value chain by contrasting complex systems against operations steps.

Learning and Growth

As one of the balanced scorecard's major four pillars, learning and growth (L&G) is aligned with the firm's strategic objectives. The purpose is to identify cause and effect linkages from the execution of daily activities concerning L&G for the organization and its employees. The focus would be on the firm's employees, their skills, satisfaction, motivation, innovation, and productivity. These attributes precondition process improvements, customer satisfaction, and ultimately financial success.

Given awareness of how business processes should operate, L&G of employees should unite with their knowledge and skills, the organizational culture, incentives, and the use of IT, to achieve optimal performance. Figure 7.2 illustrates L&G planning.

One key objective for L&G is to improve process efficiency, and then implement an IT infrastructure to make the right information available in a timely fashion (utilization of technology to provide speed and convenience to customers).

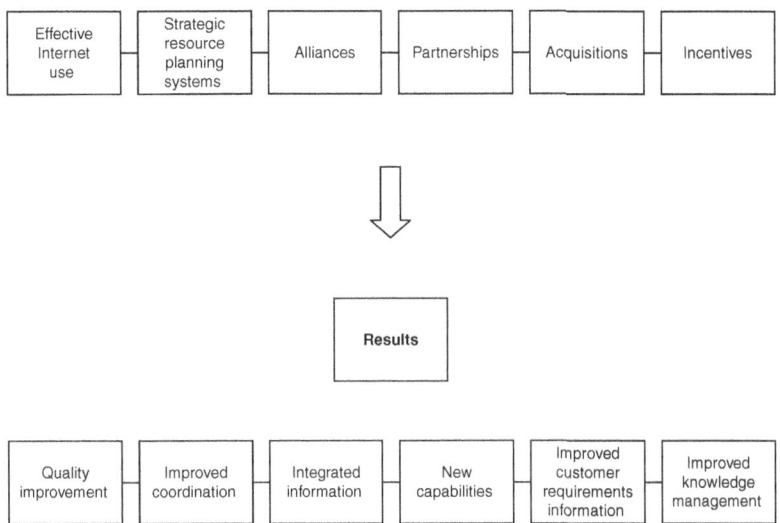

Figure 7.2   Learning and Growth Planning.

Organization development is defined in terms of innovation, managing change, and measured improvements. Resource allocation and initiatives in L&G are key processes that would create results.

Measuring employee satisfaction includes factors that the employee needs to have, which are:

- involvement with decisions;
- recognition for doing a good job;
- access to sufficient information to do the job well;
- active encouragement to be creative and use initiative;
- support level from staff functions;
- overall satisfaction with company;
- effective rewards system; and
- precise measures for accountability and responsibility.

Table 7.1 illustrates the connection between employee skills, technology, and the required actions.

Table 7.1   Value Chain Processes against Operations Steps

Staff competencies	Technology infrastructure	Climate for action
Strategic skills	Strategic technologies	Key decision cycle
Training levels	Strategic databases	Strategic focus
Skill leverage	Experience capture	Staff empowerment
	Proprietary software	Personal alignment
	Patents, trademarks	Morale, teams

The strategic business unit for L&G in terms of how to profile the market and analyze the value chain stages (source-to-customer) require key training to develop understanding of classes of trade, customers (consumer positioning), competitors, consumer segmentation (purchase decision / trade offs), and, finally, future challenges in terms of market trends and implications.

Investment Strategies

A detailed discussion of investment strategies is covered in this section. This section illustrates examples of exchange trade funds (ETFs), annuities, dividend and growth, index funds, equities, derivatives, and managing risk, to highlight what has worked following the financial crisis of 2008.

Here are ways for investors to pursue more income with low risk. Building a portfolio for growth should be laced with funds that are geared for long-term records and a diverse mix of assets, such as broad bond and equity funds that provide for both income and diversification. In addition, the possibility of owning an all-in-one fund that invests in both bonds and stocks and tactically shifts to take advantage of changing market conditions should be a serious consideration. Demand for fixed-income investment has pushed yields lower for many categories such as the treasury's, investment grade corporate stocks, and junk bonds. Prices and yields move in opposite directions in bond markets. High-quality bonds become vulnerable to retrenchment as a gradual pick up in economic growth poses the risk of higher inflation.

Commodities ETFs, rather than tracking spot prices, is linked to prices of future contracts, and performance can diverge from the spot price as funds roll their holdings from one contract to another. ETFs usually target both frontier and emerging markets. In general, a frontier market is at an earlier stage of development than an emerging market. Strategic income bond funds invest in many sectors and have considerable flexibility to adjust holdings to reduce risk or to take advantage of opportunities. They often have a portion of the portfolio in lower-rated bonds, where prices can fluctuate during periods of volatility, but they usually are less vulnerable than funds that make more concentrated wagers. Fund managers usually have been adept at repositioning by trimming exposure to high-yield and emerging market bonds before they get into a downward shift. They would reverse as valuations become more attractive.

Recently, the fund industry has introduced more all-in-one strategies, which often are conservative allocation funds. These funds own bonds, stocks, and other securities that generate attractive income including Master Limited Partnerships (MLPs), which usually are backed by energy pipelines that generate regular revenue under longer term contracts. This revenue is then passed on to investors. The managers of conservative allocation funds consistently adjust exposure to capitalize on developments in various market areas, such as ETFs.

Financial firms offer a dizzying variety of ETFs that generate attractive yields from both broad and narrow portfolios. A key advantage is that ETFs typically charge lower fees than traditional funds, which translates to higher returns to investors. ETFs usually have a mix in equities and investment-grade bonds. They also may include high-yield bonds and real estate securities. An ETF mix could employ assets that rest in a range of investment-grade bonds and dividend-paying stocks to emerging market bonds. ETF managers primarily invest in dividend-paying stocks, but also buy MLPs, real estate investment trusts (REITs), and US and foreign bonds.

Over time, a balance that looks for price gains as well as yield is a stronger premise for investments. This refers to incomecash flow—such as the money generated by bond interest payments or stock dividends, with lower interest rates and falling bond yields. It is unlikely that portfolios can generate as much pure income. Nonetheless, investors need to rely on a total return strategy that promotes cash flow and capital appreciation by building equity. The total return strategy aims for enough appreciation to make the money last longer. One important advantage of total-return strategy is that it makes it easier to spread risk. The holdings are not required to pay out significant current income, but build capital over time, which allows for adding many types of stocks and other securities to the mix. Over longer-term investment periods, most bonds provide no protection against inflation. Stocks offer some inflation insurance because under most circumstances, their prices will appreciate along with economic growth, with some providing for rising dividends as well.

Conservative investors should always balance the potential income from securities against the risk of price declines that would offset or exceed the payouts. For example, long-term bonds generally pay higher interest than short-term ones. However, for any given rise in interest rates, they will fall much more sharply in price.

Although a balanced portfolio starts with stocks and bonds, it should not end there. Investors are discovering that they are less diversified than they were considered to be. The global economy is creating an interconnected world whereby portfolios may benefit from assets that did not always move with stocks and bonds, for example, currencies, commodities, gold, and real estate. Globalizing thinking is important to investment strategies as it relates to US stocks, bonds, foreign stocks, and alternatives such as ETFs that might link to emerging markets. It is very notable that investments in securities of mining and metal companies may be speculative and may be subject to volatility. Investments in real estate companies, including REITs, are subject to volatility and risk, including loss of value, which may be attributed to poor management, lowered credit ratings, among other factors. Similar real estate investment companies may also be subject to liquidity risks. On the other hand, currency derivatives investments may be particularly volatile. Commodity-linked investments are considered speculative and therefore have substantial risks, including the loss of significant portion of their principal value. Diversification does not guarantee profit or protect against loss. Diversification should be a well-thought-out flexible plan that mitigates risk, but does not eliminate it altogether.

Annuities

Before investing, consider the funds' investment objectives, risks, charges, and expenses. Sector funds can be more volatile than the overall market because of their concentration. Industrials can be significantly affected by general economic trends, and changes in consumer sentiments and spending. In addition, commodity prices, legislation, government regulation and spending, import controls, and worldwide competition can be subject to liability for environmental damage, depletion of resources, and mandated expenditures for safety and pollution control.

For years, the only option for fixed-income annuity was the immediate annuity. Purchasers could pay a lump sum for an insurance contract that guaranteed usually monthly payments that started shortly thereafter and lasted the rest of the life of the contract. Recently, insurance companies came out with a new fixed-income product, longevity insurance, which delays payout until the buyers are in their expected last decade of survival. These type of contracts assumed too much liability and did not sell well.

Alternatively, insurers have introduced annuities that start making fixed payouts in just five to ten years. Many middle-aged people bought into these products to substitute pensions to help supplement their income at the very outset of their retirement. Annuities can provide a guaranteed income stream. A big question remains: How should annuities affect the rest of the portfolio?

With variable annuities, investors can allow for increased risk and exposure at the benefit of higher return. Fixed payment annuities could involve risk if the issuer is on shaky ground, or if the annuity lacks automatic increases to protect against inflation.

A hybrid, fixed-index annuity has been emphasized recently as a guardian against fluctuations in the stock market. They guarantee that the principal value remains the same even if the market has a major downfall. If the market is flat, the principal value is protected. Nonetheless, if the market goes up, then additional interests are paid and the principal value increases. Contracts are drawn similar to fixed annuities based on five-to-ten-year payouts. Figure 7.3 reflects the hybrid annuity index as reported by the American Equity's Index-5.

The global economic melt down of 2008, which affected all financial markets, demonstrated the value of guaranteed income from annuities to their owners—and the financial danger to the insurance companies. While most insurers ran hedging those risks, as markets slid, many insurers had to set up

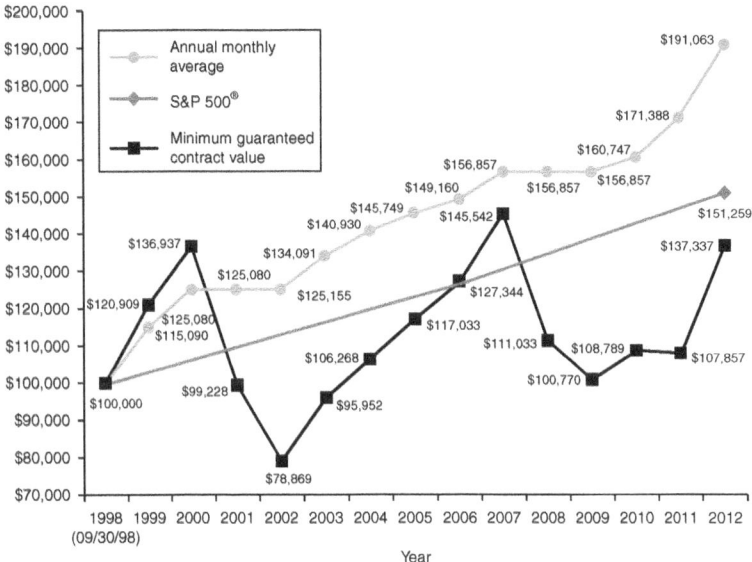

Figure 7.3   Hybrid Annuity Index Performance.

bigger reserves for the guarantees, which hurt earnings. They also raised capital totaling billions of dollars, which diluted shareholders' stakes, to show regulators that they can keep commitments to their customers. Some of these insurers had to take government aid, since repaid insurers' stocks continued to be depressed by the exposure they faced from payout guarantees. The main risk remains if the insurance company holding the annuity goes out of business.

Dividend and Growth

Wireless smart phones and exploding Internet technologies created additional pressure on investing into technology stocks whereby investing for income and investing in technology are not mutually exclusive anymore. Previously, all investments in technology stocks were based on growth in these stocks without any expectations for any dividend income. The fast-paced, high-stakes technology sector is one of the biggest contributors to dividends in the Standard & Poor 500 stock index. Besides the fact that technology stocks are a larger sector in this benchmark, they also represent about 20 percent of the stock market value. Titan companies such as Apple Inc. and Cisco Systems Inc. are now paying shareholder payouts. As such, a number of technology-oriented mutual funds (MFs) and ETFs have joined the ranks of dividend payers.

These technology dividend paying companies are not used to this new doctrine. They may not be committed to annual increases as a traditional company such as one dealing with consumer products; for example, Procter & Gamble and Coca Cola raised dividends for over half a century. The technology company paying of dividends is a leap of faith as most of the companies in this sector reinvested all their profits into growth in many areas of their business.

Many of these companies wanted the affluence of growth rather than showing that they have grown up. Cash is plowed into the business to spur growth for research and development, acquisitions, and grabbing market share from competitors.

The fear of paying dividend might also be perceived as indicating that the company ran out of growth potential. Growth investors look at dividend as the company cannot reinvest the money back into growing the business to get a higher rate of return based on equity. Cash machines such as semiconductor giant Intel corp. and networking leader Cisco pay dividends because their core business is mature, irrespective of massive efforts to reinvent into product development. Although Apple accepted the fact that the global economy has faced slowdown since 2008 until 2012, they continue to expand their products in the smart wireless technologies irrespective of fewer avenues for growth. As companies become more mature, it does not mean that their growth prospects have ended. Growth companies that are innovative can strike a balance between maturity and pay dividends, but continue to invest into developmental technologies to ensure growth horizon potentials. Shareholders desire and respond to dividend payouts and can be leery of growth promises unless a company introduces new products that have potential for major profit.

ETFs and Index Funds

Index funds are wrongly and generally assumed that turnover costs are not significant. While it is generally accepted that low turnover is a hallmark of broad market indexes such as the S&P 500 index, funds that track them shuffle their components extensively, which can lead to higher expenses and reduced returns. In addition, turnover also can increase when index funds change their benchmarks as recently observed by Vanguard Group's plan to execute some of its ETFs. The cost of turnover is incurred as a fund sells some holdings and buys others. The fund accounts for these tradings, but withholds the amount that has been paid as commission in such obscure transactions that have hard-to-estimate market prices and bid-asking spreads when the trades are executed.

Some indexes are in a constant state of flux. Indexes of short-term securities, for example, treasury bills, constantly move components that are maturing and replace them with new ones. Commodity indexes, which track futures contracts with definite life span, do the same. Equities indexes, on the other hand, attempt to beat the broad market by shuffling their holdings extensively. The Securities and Exchange Commission (SEC) has a formula for calculating turnover that funds must follow: the lesser of purchases or sales divided by the average assets in the fund over a specified time period, usually one year. Many prospectuses for trust funds warn investors about high turnover costs. These costs might not be reflected in annual funds operating expenses, which hit costs on returns.

Benchmark changes are likely to impact turnover. Portfolios get transitioned from one index to another, for example, transitioning from London FTSE and US benchmark to other measures. In general, emerging market funds will have higher turnover. An index measure can vary based on the assumption of a specific market. US measure is about 15 percent weight in South Korean stocks, while the FTSE index has zero percent weight because the FTSE classifies South Korea as a developed market.

Most index providers try to curtail turnover while ensuring that their indexes continue to reflect market reality. Major turnover issues show up in market segment indexes such as those for large and small stocks or growth and value ones. Buffer zones between adjacent segments are the most common form of turnover control. For example, a small stock with growing market value will be moved to the large-stock index only after it penetrates the large stock by 10 to 20 percent in value.

Actively managed MFs' high turnover can indicate potential capital gains for investors. In contrast, ETFs with high turnover stock portfolios have not paid capital-gain distributions in recent years. This is because ETFs can export a lot of trading activities to brokerage firms through the creation of other redemption avenues. When money flows into an ETF, the money manager issues a request for creation units, which are made of stocks that replicate the ETF holding on a smaller scale. The major holders of ETFs exchange these units for shares in the ETFs. When money flows out, redemption units replace securities in exchange for ETF shares. By carefully managing these processes, most of the trading that triggers capital gains or losses takes place away from the ETFs' portfolio.

Fundamentals of Industry Analysis

Equities

The goal of this type of analysis is to get an insight into the companies in significant business areas. This analysis would target offering comprehensive data, trend analysis, thematic perspective, and functionality of dashboards in the specific industry sector. Equities are dependent on the size of the market, main competitors, basic drivers such as future goodwill, and key metrics that include debt to equity financial ratios.

Derivatives

Betting on rates with options is used by investors to swap in the market by trying to profit from interest-rate shifts. There is a major difference between equity options and interest-rate options in terms of the payoff structure. A purchased traditional equity call option grants the right to buy a stock at a set strike price. The payoff at expiration is the maximum price minus the strike price. If the stock price is higher than the strike, the option pays the difference. If the stock price is lower than the strike, the option expires with no value. Interest rate options are more complex. Fixed percent interest rate is agreed to for the duration, typically three to five years, for about 5 percent. An investor agrees to buy the right to pay 5 percent fixed interest annually on the 3–5 years contract. At expiration, that is, at the end of 5 years, if the swap interest rate is higher than 5 percent, then the swaption is in the money and the investor would be able to exercise. The payoff is equal to the difference between the prevailing swap interest rate and the set rate in the contract period.

Risk

One can gauge the health of the financial system and identify potential pitfalls by studying the data released by the US Federal

Reserve board on a regular basis. The FED released detailed guidelines related to lending programs it put in place in 2008 to alleviate the subprime financial meltdown. Professionals who follow financial information regularly published by the US central bank would have already concluded that foreign banks were huge borrowers during the crisis. Needed liquidity pushed these banks to borrow based on the fact that the European banking system relies on bank-to-bank lending rather than having a lender of last resort. While money was more available in the US banking system then, the European banking system was under stress. It made sense for European banks to turn to the US market, where the cost of cash was cheaper and readily available.

Market watchers who follow the FED increase their chances of avoiding losses should another debacle unfold. To spot strains in the financial market, one would track trading in the federal funds rate—the amount that banks charge each other for overnight loans. When this rate veers sharply from the FED target level (as it did in 2008), that would be an indication of risk. Banks tap the FED when they cannot get funding from other lenders. This also is an indication of risk as it shows stress or an inability for banks to get funded in the open market. The FED loans are available to all banks that are members in the Federal Reserve system. To be a member and have that privilege, the banks must leave a percentage of cash at the FED every two weeks. This money earns no interest and is available to the FED "free" to use.

8

Innovation versus Invention

Henry Ford, who started his own revolution a century ago, once said: "History is more or less bunk. It is tradition. We do not want tradition. We want to live in the present, and the only history that is worth a tinker's damn is the history we make today." Like Ford, today's partisans of the new economy, rightly, can be criticized for an oversized sense of their own uniqueness: Never before had technology been so transforming such that the laws of economics are being challenged.

The task of preparing for the genuinely unknowable future that faced Meriwether Lewis, as he sought to organize his exploration of a route to the Pacific, was that he was acutely aware of the importance of talent. His operating principles could be summarized as he stated: "Pick your people as if your life depends on it—because it might very well might."

Michael Porter spoke of how competitive forces shape strategy. He analyzed competitive forces such as threat of entry into a business. He highlighted barriers to entry as economies of scale, product differentiation, capital requirement, cost advantages irrespective of size, access to distribution channels, and government policy. Competitors jockey for power by enlisting bargaining power of their suppliers or scheduled customers. They even highlight substitution of products such as transistors replacing tubes, CDs replacing vinyl records, high fructose corn syrup replacing sugar, or vegetable oil replacing corn oil. One major impact is in the pharmaceutical industry where generic drugs replace branded drugs upon patent expiration. The rivals are diverse in strategy and have various ideas about how to compete among each other.

Front-to-End manufacturing

The essence of strategy is to perform activities differently than rivals do. At a leading pharmaceutical manufacturing company dealing in specialty novel products, the following strategies were developed and executed:

1. As a company, we are committed to total quality management; we emphasize a premier work environment such that the work (projects, batch or continuous process, assembly, etc.) has significant implications for the entire organization, including signature of quality that certifies our products, forecasting, layout, equipment selection and maintenance, process and inventory control, efficient material handling and on-time delivery. We strive to integrate quality in every aspect of what we do, and to continuously optimize costs.

2. We pay attention to variability in production or service rates. We recognize that any of these can adversely affect customer satisfaction and costs. We avoid "certainty traps" by building appropriate flexibility into our systems to ensure effective response to change. Our organization greatly emphasizes how managers relate to subordinates, which has tremendous implications on the success of our executions. Selection, training, motivation, and support are all important values that govern our operations.

3. We are at the front end of our core technology and dedicated to paying attention to details in our know-how. We consider both the opportunities and risks that influence our path: improvements in quality, services, and response time. Technology can be

costly, difficult to integrate, and requires upgrades, which might hinder progress when technology is newly introduced. However, with our focus on steady state process we tend to benefit from the eventual results. Along the way, we never underestimate our competitors and we always assume that they make the best decisions. We also understand that in making decisions, tradeoffs are involved. We follow our path and constantly strive to perform our business in the most ethical manner.

Enterprise Resource Planning

An increasing number of firms recognize that they must continue to invest in innovative technology in order to gain a strategic advantage in today's business environment. Companies are faced with the challenge of keeping pace with the economic changes and developments within their respective industries. This struggle for a strategic edge is even more pressing due to the growing global business arena. Many companies are finding that they need instant, consolidated worldwide information with minimal support effort. One technology currently in the business world helping companies achieve this goal is a multimillion-dollar system called enterprise resource planning (ERP).

ERP is a software system that links and integrates all functional areas and operating locations of a business. Companies such as SAP, Oracle, PeopleSoft, J. D. Edwards, Baan, and Lawson have developed an expertise in this area. Each offers its own ERP product. Its goal is to increase performance, productivity, and profitability throughout any organization. ERP systems provide benefits including improved information sharing and business process improvement. However, to get there on the road is a costly and lengthy implementation. In addition, there is usually a severe culture shock experienced by the people in an organization once ERP is implemented. Despite these issues, there is a growing cadre of ERP users, particularly in the

Fortune 500 companies. As the trend of using enterprise-wide computing systems continues, ERP providers will find themselves constantly challenged to provide innovative products and services to their customers.

ERP systems allow for a more efficient distribution of information and effective approach to data management. Specifically, ERP solutions improve upon timeliness of information and operations, consistency and accuracy of information, and controlled access to that information. The ERP systems improve these areas by amounts that were previously unheard of in the business world. Such promises of improvements are especially enticing because these areas are also often identified as key problem areas within many organizations. An example of a specific improvement is in the consistency of information. ERP systems maintain one main information storage that is accessed, used, and updated by all of the separate functional areas of the business such as manufacturing, human resources, accounting, and customer service. Each major functional area of the business operates its own module of software that is tied into the main ERP system. For example, the accounting department would be utilizing a financial module of the ERP system while the customer service department would be using an order management module. However, both departments would be accessing the same underlying data source. This enterprise-wide access ensures that every person within the entire organization is looking at and using the same information. The different modules, or software applications, are designed to work with the main ERP system. Therefore, while the type of information and the presentation of each module may be very different, each and every module is still using the same information store.

Additionally, with one source of information, the speed with which that information can be accessed and processed improves immensely. Time-consuming data transfers and compilations by hand, due to the all-too-common problem of software incompatibility across an organization, are no longer necessary. In addition, with this one source, information is easier to interpret and organize so that the right person is getting the right output. In this light, each level of management can access and update that information that is most meaningful to them, in a format that is designed for them, without waiting for one or more other department(s) to provide it.

Another area that ERP systems improve upon is controlled access to information. One consistent security control system can be set in place because there is only one data source. No matter at what level of management you are, or at what operating site or area you may be, the security clearance is treated the same and only you are permitted access to information that pertains to you. The other side of this access coin is that the data that the employee is accessing can be tailored specifically for them. Each level of management is able to have only the information presented to them that is pertinent and useful to their operational responsibilities.

An example of all of these improved aspects working together can be seen when an employee at a foreign division of a company fulfills a customer's quote request for a product that is only made in the US division. Under the previous decentralized business system, this employee would have to get in touch with someone to determine available stock, another person to provide available delivery schedule dates, and yet another person to determine the price if the product is customer specific, etc. Each of these contacts would take a few days to get the information. The original employee must then compile this information for presentation to the customer, by which time some or all of the information is most likely already outdated. With an ERP system in place, however, the scenario would be dramatically different. That employee would be able to access the main database of information and retrieve accurate inventory numbers, schedule availability, pricing information, etc. He would also be able to request this data in a format that is ready to be presented to the customer. From this example, it is easy to visualize how much of an advantage an ERP system can offer any company.

Finally, a primary advantage touted by ERP vendors is that implementing an ERP system triggers business process improvement throughout the company. For example, the typical organization is divided into departments that perform different functions for the common goal of generating profit for company growth. Each of these departments tends to use their own unique software applications. Although these software packages work very well within their particular department, they are not well suited for other departments or the company as a whole. Since each department wants to use its own applications, the different applications would then need to be integrated if the data were to travel between departments. Traditionally, the average corporation spends close to one-third of its IT budget on integrating applications. Today, however, ERP systems offer a much more efficient and effective way to overcome this integration nightmare. Furthermore, while planning the integration process, the business workflow is reviewed and analyzed. Again, this is where key process improvements occur. The organization must look to cut out inefficient processes along with developing new "best practices" to allow the company to fully utilize the enhanced integrated systems technology.

Unfortunately, ERP does come with several drawbacks. First of all, an implementation can involve millions. Then there is the cost of continuous system upgrades in addition to the maintenance. Second, the consulting expense for an ERP program can get outrageous due to the complexity of ERP packages and the shortage of professional consultants in the market. Their skills and output will literally be left as a footprint on the organization. Lastly, an ERP implementation can take from one to four years depending on the size of the organization and the desired functionality.

ERP implementation is a major decision for a company. Because of the extraordinary cost and time involved, it is almost impossible to switch ERP software packages once one is in place. It is just economically unfeasible to do two ERP implementations. Additionally, the businesses process reengineering, also known as "culture change," are also included in the total cost of utilizing ERP. One of the issues that seem to be contrary to ERP vendor promotions is that, typically, ERP systems do not reduce headcount. The culture change that results also includes a requirement for a more sophisticated user base. These "super-users" utilized during implementation become essential to the continuous maintenance of the program; many never return full-time to their original positions. Another critical point for a successful implementation is that management must commit to changes in the working environment. For example, they now have to share data that they previously secured in their own system or cabinet. However, the new information flow within an ERP-enabled organization facilitates creation of cross-functional management, which is more efficient. The new organization will have global access to real-time information. ERP offers consistent control of business processes, and facilitates steps for allowing the enterprise to focus more on its fundamental economic tasks.

The ERP Industry

The ERP market currently has several key vendors providing integrated systems to the corporate environment. These major players include Baan, J. D. Edwards, Lawson Software, Oracle, PeopleSoft, and SAP. Their products range from basic financial packages to providing manufacturing management applications.

Systems, Applications, and Products in Data Processing (SAP) and Oracle deliver scalable client/server enterprise application software that enables its customers to improve upon their best business practices. Their system has modules that support business functions in the financial, manufacturing, sales and distribution, and human resources areas.

Oracle and SAP are the largest suppliers of ERP software today. They promote the theory of "best business practices" by providing a choice of ready-made business processes. Their technology partners are leading vendors such as IBM, Hewlett-Packard, Sun, Intel, and others. In addition, they have many consulting partners globally that help them provide consulting capabilities worldwide. Many of these partners include Accenture Consulting, Cap Gemini, Ernst & Young, Deloitte & Touche, and others. One of ERP's weaknesses is that there is usually a lengthy implementation process. In addition, customization for individual modules is complex and can be very expensive. They have led the market in the new supply chain management applications.

Facing challenges, ERP firms are searching for new business opportunities that will help keep them growing. ERP firms are looking at the front office arena now that back-end systems, such as accounting, manufacturing, and human resources, have been reengineered. They are beginning to expand into Customer Relationship Management (CRM) software. Another direction that ERP firms are pursuing is the outsourcing or rental of ERP applications. Moreover, major ERP vendors are jumping on the Internet / e-commerce bandwagon by either offering middleware to link to their ERP software or providing direct links to their products. Finally, they are making strategic decisions on how they work with the other half of the ERP team, the consultants who actually implement the software, from making exclusive partnerships to bringing the work in-house.

The simplest definition of CRM is a souped up Sales Force Automation (SFA) software. Whereas SFA applications manage contacts, accounts, and sales opportunities, CRM includes front-office applications that deal with customers; adds customer, product information, and advertising material; throws in marketing literature and product configuration models; and has the ability to hook to back-end systems. Like ERP, CRM is meant to free sales from administrative details and allow them to concentrate on the important job of spending more quality time with customers so that sales will increase.

Overall, the benefits of ERP systems with integrated software modules covering the gamut of business management functions have been well received in the commercial world. Although the road to ERP involves hurdles such as cost and lengthy implementation, there are documented results that there is a "measurable payback" in financial benefits. With the ever-increasing pressure to innovate in the information technology field, ERP vendors will find that they must continue to discover new and improved products and services to help customers maintain a competitive advantage.

Installing an ERP system generally reflects the beginning of a new way of organizational life.

Reinvention—Successes and Failures

Customers often slip through your fingers when, instead of offering innovative new products, you try to lock them into older ones that do not present the added features of perceived benefits. Oracle learned that while following plans to acquire software specialist Taleo, which provides customer relationship software over the Internet that is opposed to "on-premise" software solutions that are a specialty of both Oracle and SAP. The market is moving toward more "cloud" solutions over the Internet that are provided through companies like Right-Now, Salesforce.com, and Work-day. Nonetheless, customers continue to pay high maintenance fees to the likes of Oracle, as they need to put up with high prices because it is painful to rip out ERP software.

Eastman Kodak Co. got into the business of picture making with the slogan, "You press the button, we do the rest," more than a century ago. Kodak stopped making cameras, digital cameras, and digital picture frames, which were the heart of its foundation. This decision is the strongest symbol of the sea change in consumer electronics, which emphasizes that missteps can force a blue chip icon to seek bankruptcy protection. As a photography icon, Kodak lost its stronghold on film and camera markets. This is living proof for companies to continue investing in innovation for survival purposes. Digital technologies had cannibalized businesses of slow movers who did not adjust to customer requirements and demands, as digital technology replaced the need for film, and smartphones deeply dented the demand for digital cameras.

On the other hand, innovators like Apple continue to build value for their stakeholders and customers. Apple is updating Mac software, and making it available to developers. The updates include messaging service, notifications applications, gaming center, sharing and integrating with company on-line services, iCloud (on-line remote storage-and-syncing application, etc., which were all pioneered for the iPad and iPhone, which use software known as iOS. It appears that all these technologies are on a convergence path to satisfy consumer needs in every aspect of behavior. In addition, Apple is addressing the global market, for example, by creating new hooks to popular Chinese Internet services, like the search service Baidu Inc., while keeping Google as the search default.

As many original innovators lost their path, others were able to adjust to market shifts and start innovating in related technologies building on fundamentals that they learned in basic mainstream businesses. Milliken and Co. of South Carolina arguably could have been crushed like many others in the textile business when cheaper textiles flooded the US market from abroad. Its roots were in the labor-intensive textile industry that long ago decamped for lower wages abroad from global competition. Milliken diversified rapidly out of traditional textiles and moved into niche products that built off its knowledge of textiles and specialty chemicals. It focused its scientific research and manufacturing on innovation. The results are enumerated in products such as fabric that reinforces duct tape, additives for refrigerated containers, washable markers, fire-resistant coatings for mattresses, antimicrobial laminates, and protective combat gear, among other products. It amassed a solid portfolio of patents focusing on specialty fabrics, floor coverings, specialty chemicals, and performance-based products. Milliken was different because of their willingness to change in a fast manner. This transformation based on innovation created quality leadership through research. They maintain a high-caliber staff with advanced degrees in the various related sciences and engineering. They created a culture that rewards innovation by allowing their researchers to follow their curiosity to a marketable end.

Fujifilm thrived by changing focus. As photographic film relegated to the margins in the forerunner years of digital expansion, Fujifilm transformed from a fairly narrow photographic supplier into a diversified company with significant health care and electronic operations. Both Fujifilm and Kodak knew that the digital age was surging; they made different decisions. Fujifilm decided to look further than simply moving to digital photography from analog. Instead, Fujifilm tapped its chemical expertise for broader uses, such as drugs and liquid crystal display (LCD) panels. Fujifilm ventured into cosmetics using nonfading technologies for skin applications. This transformation was not easy in terms of changes to the workforce and cost-cutting measures. They managed to employ technologies originally developed for photography into other fields. The ultrathin layers, which contain about a hundred compounds, were utilized to engineer films used in LCD panels for computers, TV sets, and other screen devices. Fujifilm became a leading competitive supplier of film to LCD-panel component suppliers. Fujifilm also ventured into drugs, seeking ways to increase the human body absorption of chemical elements in drugs. They acquired many health care companies, and made a foray into anti-aging skin care products based on antioxidation technology for preventing photos from fading. Its reported income from photo film is less than 1 percent of its business.

Integrating Operations ERP and Total Quality Management Systems in Marketing Strategy

Supply Chain Management would be optimal when customers' forecast is integrated in a comprehensive supplier-to-customer wrap around relationship that is configured on a 24/7 order capture that is carried based on far-sighted strategic analysis that ensures on-time delivery to meet customer demand.

Leading manufacturers look at the purchasing, manufacturing, and customer service as the three prongs of the integrated supply chain. Design controls within research and development, manufacturing engineering, and quality controls within quality assurance should all be integrated in a material requirement plan to ensure that supplies are available for manufacturing. Inventories should be optimal to prevent tying assets for a longer term. This means that the various links within an organization when optimized through an automated ERP system will ensure the profitability and flow of products within the organization.

This is simply the value chain that links all suppliers to an organization and provides superior service and quality products to its customers.

With the emphasis on customer satisfaction and efficient customer response, organizations are faced with the challenge of quick change to respond to customer needs. As the organization grows, more and more systems that are based on policies and procedures are needed. These Standard Operating procedures (SOPs) need to be linked through an integrated enterprise resources planning system utilizing methodical approaches that ensure product quality by effectively linking all departmental activities at optimal costs. This would ensure that all existing product improvements, line extensions, or new product introductions serviced by the business marketing plan meets the requirements of the marketing strategy.

Companies need to maintain a competitive advantage (Porter, 1985) despite economic cycles. It is critical to step outside the box, focus on the bigger picture, and become involved in resource allocation and management. A company strategy should engage concepts that incorporate continuous improvement (Kaplan, 1996) such that a company will emerge as a dominant player in the industry. Besides efficient manufacturing systems, the movement of products and services in a well-integrated logistical system that ensures fast distribution, transportation, and warehousing are linked through an enterprise management system is crucial to the success of the entire operation. Transformation of manufacturing practices to manage complexity with processes that are more reliable, managing the supply chain to secure control of global shipments, and enabling new business by using leading-edge technologies should all be well connected in the enterprise system.

A totally integrated inventory management solution would require a system from the point of use to replenishment, with information access at anytime (Lanning, 1998). This system would notify the supplier to restock, enabling the company to maintain optimal inventory levels to meet customer demand.

Improvements in the purchasing cost structure and processes can bring very quick gains. Companies operate in a very competitive environment, with constant pressure to contain costs while continually trimming cycle time and improving service. The pressure is on to reduce lead times for customers. From purchase orders to blanket orders, companies are constantly stepping up their effort to keep inventory levels low. More advanced companies are having their material resource planning requirements transmitted electronically to suppliers (Judge, 1998). The key is to communicate net weekly factory demands to the chain supply resulting in lower inventory levels and improved supplier capacity utilization. Moving from one-year contract to longer contracts with suppliers enables the company to lock in better price breaks and manifold reductions in lead times. In addition, if the company starts to receive longer-term forecasts from its customers, then this would enable weekly or biweekly scheduled shipments from ship-to-stock programs.

There are two important business premises that tie-in marketing strategy to the need for efficient supply chain to provide value to the customer in the business world today:

1. We need to change faster than the changes that take place outside our own walls. Otherwise, it is a matter of time before we lose our competitive edge.
2. The control of a business future will be inherited by the fastest learning organization.

Change is not easy. It requires behavior modifications (Hammer, 1993). Usually people do not complain when the change creates a convenience to them. Therefore, how can we get employees engaged so that they see change as a convenience?

Treating people with dignity, respect, and integrity is the bedrock of TQM. Engaging people through these values is the best way to drive TQM. Engaging people requires empowering them by getting their inputs. Empowering people does not mean leaders relinquish their responsibilities. It means that they establish goals, anchor the organization to a set of values, and give employees the necessary tools and skills to operate within these parameters. When employees are integrated into the inputs to the organization, their involvement means that they can manage change and foster continuous learning, which are required for market place success. When leaders and employees are connected and they are empowered, you ultimately make customers happy because they feel the pride, enthusiasm, passion, and energy in the employees' actions. Only then, the company wins in the marketplace.

Managing the supplier base is important for a company that seeks consolidation of many suppliers to reduce its current vendors with the goal of forming strategic partnerships. Assessing a current supplier base is key to a company's evaluation of suppliers' capabilities, and the next step is comparing that to the various components and parts that the company has to buy. Suppliers are evaluated for financial stability, technical competence, demonstrated quality requirements, flexibility regarding scheduling and inventory, and price competitiveness. In addition, companies are interested in suppliers who are willing to maintain a certain level of contingency or buffer inventory in their facility. The ultimate goal is to set up a one-stop shop by entering into strategic partnerships with selected suppliers. Companies would be interested in suppliers who have in-built capabilities to provide integrated assemblies as an added value supply (benefit) rather than just the components.

Longer-term forecasts allow the supplier to deliver directly to stations on the factory floor based on preset factory-defined supply quantities (Kanban). Suppliers issue monthly invoices against their deliveries which helps streamline administrative tasks.

Companies should work on delegating inspection authority to certified suppliers. Certification allows a company to investigate a supplier's internal control mechanism, training, inspection equipment, and criteria, such that the vendor meets all the necessary requirements.

Progressive companies today use supplier management as an effective strategy. At its highest level, supplier management is about achieving the best-landed cost from a mix of strategic and nonstrategic suppliers with the information that enables the corporation to provide excellent products and services. Optimizing the full set of suppliers based on the company relationships requires more than just reducing the number of vendors in a company's supplier base. While reducing the supplier base may be a key objective, buyers need to balance the risk of downtime and build some contingencies to protect supply. Effective supply management requires the following:

1. Get a complete integrated look at the purchasing across the company including buying done by divisions or plants.
2. Identify strategic suppliers and value-added products against commodities and nonstrategic suppliers.
3. Classify suppliers based on their strategic relationships. Ensure that the business process supports these choices.
4. Purchase and install home-grown enabling technology.

Purchasing used to focus on material costs: selling price, getting the lowest unit cost, and negotiating the best price. Companies have transitioned to consider total landed cost. This means considering not only how much a specific unit costs, but also considering other factors such as delivery, and who will manage inventory. Purchasing managers are charged with the responsibility of not only the cost of goods, but also planning, sourcing, and managing the total cost of the items. Procurement is evolving from a back-end transaction or administrative function to an upstream strategic function (purchasing; a new paradigm). Involvement of purchasing in product development and strategic issues at hand involves exploiting purchasing technology, and thereby procurement people will have to become supply chain oriented. Investing in productivity tools as well as in persuasive, persistent, and creative supply chain personnel requires a selling orientation of the fact that they want to enjoy a competitive advantage from suppliers so their company can win in the marketplace. Besides chasing down cost and expenses, ensuring continuity of supply and recognizing the competitive advantages that can be gained by getting new products to market on time gain greater importance, as opposed to getting to market with the lowest cost set of components. Buyers should be perceived as professionals managing a chain of suppliers with a product portfolio rather than people who handle purchase requisitions and orders. A world-class procurement function needs to be highly integrated with the entire supply and value chain.

Increased awareness should be placed on the impact transportation can have on total cost of goods. Many companies typically bundle inbound transportation cost into the delivered pricing. Most of them pay attention to the transportation cost of outbound finished goods, and focus less on inbound goods transport cost. Significant savings would be found in inbound transportation cost. Therefore, expertise within the purchasing function should target and deal with inbound transportation and logistics. Better transportation tools available now give companies the capabilities of managing more complexity. Collaboration to eliminate empty miles makes better use of transportation capacity. In addition, collaboration to eliminate an entire distribution echelon has even greater potential.

The most common dedicated contract model involves moving finished goods into a distribution network. The benefit is a highly precise pickup and delivery schedule, tailored specifically to the buyer's need. This type of dedicated service is most common in the food service industry, with deliveries to food chains such as McDonalds, Pizza Hut, or grocery stores. A second model calls for the coordinated movement of raw materials or finished goods through a network that directly adjoins the locations of other raw materials or supplies. This type of dedicated contract combines precision delivery schedules and reduces empty miles.

Successful dedicated contract is not just about hauling freight. It is about providing and receiving quality service that is consistent with the supply chain requirements. One dedicated contract user is Denso, which is a company that transports auto parts between plants in the United States and Mexico. Denso consolidates components of auto parts in Tennessee. It builds full truckloads, and then sends the parts to Mexico where final assembly is completed. The finished automotive parts are then delivered to major automotive plants in the United States.

Ryder Systems Inc., an integrated logistics and transportation management solutions provider, uses dedicated contract carriage to build relationships with customers. Ryder service supports customers with both basic and sophisticated logistics and transportation needs, including routing and scheduling. Ryder's customers want the flexibility and convenience of a private fleet while remaining isolated from the issues associated with day-to-day operations. The direct contract option facilitates the management and scheduling of routes that allows Ryder to deliver products in a more timely and efficient manner.

Companies are trying to move away from purchase orders when it comes to maintenance, office supplies, and materials repair operations (MRO). Eliminating purchase orders and telephone calls would be more efficient when it comes to a steady supply requirement. Purchasing cards would be used in these instances, which would facilitate a credit purchase. The company receives a single monthly invoice for all the purchases in the MRO system.

Some commodity supplies might be in high demand on occasions that would create manufacturing shortages. A central electronic source (Quinn, 1992) of supply, which procures similar types of commodities from suppliers around the world, who ship aggregated orders that are broken down to individual customers, would ensure continuous supplies. Channeling orders that are bought at much larger quantities gives the vendor greater leverage in the market place. The vendor would use the manufacturer's approved supply base and ensure supplies at drastically shorter lead times. Creating opportunities through new relationships with different OEMs is usually presented when dealing with a network supplier. Measuring achievement through a singular event is not conducive to continuous success. However, repeated achievements through a network vendor would transform procurement into a strategic weapon to gain competitive advantage.

Contract management or outsourcing (Garrett, 1994) has been a major development in the manufacturing of certain components or parts that are manufactured at a vendor's or contract manufacturer's site for better cost benefit. Purchasing people now have to consider dealing with a commodity item or a niche product that requires a unique relationship with suppliers who support that type of product. Outsourcing suppliers are becoming strategic partners, involved in designing and introducing a new product. Staying ahead of the price decline curve or resisting upward price pressures are significant activities. The key is to pay less than your competitors do. On the other hand, strategic buyers have a plan that details the strategic direction they are taking, spells out continuous improvement programs that they are implementing, plus plans to improve supplier quality and reduce material cost. Purchasing agents take steps to maintain continuity of supply. They consider options that include designing technology from the right set of suppliers, identifying suppliers with good manufacturing yields, double or triple sourcing, and using industry standard components that are more widely available. Establishing long-term agreements with suppliers can provide collateral and equity for the suppliers that create stronger supplier commitments resulting in more competitive pricing for the customer.

A company conducts a customer value analysis to reveal the company's strengths and weaknesses relative to various competitors. Customers are asked about what attributes they look for in choosing a product. Quantitative assessments of these attributes play a key role in identifying segments that are important for product positioning. In addition, customers are determining factors in assessing how a company's product is perceived against competitive products in the same category. These customer values are usually monitored over time to observe how a company's value chain is delivering on the planned marketing strategy.

Companies that focus on one small aspect of supply chain such as trucking, or warehousing, can be seen as one-dimensional. Information technology (IT) linkages can make them three-dimensional. Listening to customer needs and taking a lateral approach may even add more value to the supply chain integration. Companies should be able to proactively manage exceptions and to interface from sourcing and product development to finished goods. Time-definite services and predictability are two key parameters that are used as measures of a successful chain supply implementation. A company's business strategy should serve as tools to its customers. Chain supply path should provide visibility of company's products, monitor the ability to deal with trends, and be able to plan and react through a predictive model (Rayport, 1994). Event management should focus on using customer's business rules and economic objectives. Supplier and customer factories work in collaboration in a time-definite way for maximum efficiency. For example, APL Logistics offers NetTrac technology, which lets customers track merchandise by shipment or purchase order as it moves through the supply chain. The information can relate to a shipment's movement at any time, anywhere, and can be independent of whether APL logistics physically handles it or not. NetTrac is an inventory tool that resides on the customer's desktop. It allows for real-time access of shipment information through the web. In addition, NetTrac offers SKU product visibility, management by exception, tracking of milestones the customer wants to monitor, an archival data history going back two years, and unlimited access for the customer.

As an Inventory tool, NetTrac gives users access to customized fields that include a customer PO number, carrier bill of lading and container number, and a unique product code. Customers can review shipments, logistics, or merchandising reports, or export information to applications such as Excel spreadsheet.

Organizations may want to outsource all work that is support rather than revenue producing. For example, in the early 90s, IBM built a data processing facility in Rochester that consolidated five Eastman Kodak Co. facilities. Estimated savings through the 90s were $1 billion. The rationale offered by providers is compelling. With a predictable monthly payment, a company can solve all of the problems of running an application, outsourcing the cost of software ownership and maintenance. It simplifies difficulties usually encountered in implementations and avoids hiring and retaining IT staff to run the applications. The knowledge transfer happens seamlessly, automatically, at no additional cost, without any impact on schedule, and, above all, with lower risk. In addition, customers want someone with them after the implementation. Customers look for the ERP outsource to provide the IT infrastructure. Earlier models that began in the 90s were simply taking the data center operations and have someone else run them; the newer models offer outsourcing solutions such as an ERP application and attempts to treat it like a utility. The concept of outsourcing an application is attractive if it covers issues related to software integration. The outsourcing model would be attractive if it accommodates extensions such as advanced planning and scheduling, bar-code data collection, warehouse management, and applications in e-commerce. A company outsouring an ERP application should be treated as a strategic issue rather than a cost issue (Quinn, 1992). A company needs to evaluate the concept from the standpoint of what the value added is as opposed to what the reduction in cost is going to be. The most important feature in outsourcing would be if its added value contributes significantly to the implementation of management strategic plan.

The ultimate issue for outsourcing in any business sector is not how to do it, but rather whether to do it. A survey of 37 categories of outsourcing activities by the American Management Association revealed that 94 percent of the respondents participate in at least one category. Mostly, practice is growing in accounting and finance, purchasing, and inventory management. If the case for outsourcing does pass scrutiny, then outsourcing providers should be considered as vendors that may be judged on the basis of their value-added contribution.

Software vendors and their application service providers are suggesting personnel shortages or various cost reductions as the compelling issues in any justification process. However, at Simpson Industries, Michigan, the outsourcing solution was to establish an IT strategy to help it compete in the global automotive component market. It was designed to support the company's basic strategy of shifting the product mix to higher value-added engineered modular assemblies.

The new platform would have to integrate critical business functions such as general ledger, accounts payable through invoice-paying department, production planning, and inventory control. In addition, the desire would be to improve customer service with round-the-clock operations and customer support. Equally important would be a reduction in system downtime and improving system reliability in practice.

Outsourcing software services provides the opportunity to gain access to world-class IT skills, the latest technologies, and a shift in emphasis from controlling the IT infrastructure to gaining control over IT and business information. Quite important to a company is that outsourcing provides the ability to enhance the company's effectiveness by focusing on what the company does best.

Manufacturers are looking both upstream and downstream to improve efficiency and deliver value more effectively to customers. Many manufacturing companies can relate to Deere & Co. dilemma. Like many businesses, Deere & Co. has outsourced a significant portion of its production. As a result, Deere & Co. has grown increasingly dependent on its supplier base. Yet the suppliers' lack of flexibility and long lead times presented a problem when the division began to devise a strategy to more closely synchronize its production with seasonal demand. The dilemma is how to position the firm in the value chain. This begins with the processing of raw materials and ends when the end user is satisfactorily using a finished product. Facing this challenge starts with an examination of the company's core competencies. This evaluation will reflect on the things that the company does best in creating value for customers.

On occasions, the outcome of a value chain strategy is for a company to become less vertically integrated (Kaplan and Norton, 1996). The result is to outsource production, logistics, or other functions in the company as deemed necessary. However, outsourcing can result in loss of control over key capabilities, which in turn can affect the company's ability to introduce change in response to shifts in the marketplace. Furthermore, it limits the company's ability to improve its efficiency in serving customers. For this reason, there have been additional efforts to build collaborations to improve both the flow of materials and information through out the value chain. Extended enterprise management encompasses trade partnerships with the vendor of a company supplier and satisfaction of the client of the company's customer. Shaping a strategy that reflects the reality of the downstream marketplace often leads to new approaches to upstream supplier management.

Successful models in controlling inventory had been based on a pull-replenishment process tied to customer demand. Traditionally, companies had based their production on forecasts and pushed products to dealers or distribution channels. This required stocking for an entire season, which helped to level out factory production schedules, but led to an excessive and costly amount of finished goods in inventory, which is usually financed by the manufacturer. Despite the various available products, occasionally the distributors do not stock the items that might be in demand by the customer, which in turn creates customer dissatisfaction. Product availability is a key aspect of the customer's perception of value. Therefore, creating an order-fulfillment system that is able to provide products to the customers on a quick turnaround basis is essential to customer satisfaction. One step that a company could take to ensure fast turnaround on orders would be to establish a central distribution warehouse where a moderate level of finished goods inventory would be maintained to ensure fast and reliable delivery of products to replace those that dealers or distributors have sold. Keeping this buffer, rather than replicating inventory at multilocations enables the company to respond quickly and slash overall finished goods inventory levels by a significant amount. This replenishment-based system also requires greater flexibility at the factory level and at the suppliers' level. A change in a business process usually requires a change in the business process at the suppliers' as well. In short, extended supply chain partners behave as though they are part of a single organization. In deciding where to focus supplier development to meet a company's metric, such as manufacturing cycle time, managers recognize opportunities for cost reduction and quality improvement if a long cycle time is encountered. Moreover, working with suppliers to reduce their cycle time improves their ability to respond to changes in product mix and volumes.

Many companies recognize the importance of synchronizing the activities between multiple links in the value chain (Rayport and Sviokla, 1994). The terms "supply chain" and "value chain" are almost used interchangeably. Many executives think of supply chain as the flow of incoming materials rather than the outbound links to end customers. Typically, their attention is limited to a single connection with either an immediate supplier or a direct customer. One key difference between supply chain and value chain management is primarily based on where the emphasis is placed. Traditionally, supply chain thinking places emphasis on efficiency measures such as cost reduction or other productivity measures, whereas value chain approach is effectiveness-oriented. Companies under these measures are not necessarily trying to reduce costs as an end, but rather a means to an end, which is primarily concerned with creating the highest value for the customer, which is not always the lowest cost when quality measures are taken into consideration. For example, some companies had slashed inventories drastically to curb cost and claim efficiency, but had forgotten about product availability to satisfy their customers. The value chain would emphasize a balanced approach to offer customer solutions that truly meet customer needs, in terms of quick delivery and at lower cost levels of executing these solutions. A business marketing strategy should be based on determining the best means or best combination of channels to reach the end customer. The customer now determines on how to spend his/her money to maximize value. If they require face-to-face interactions, which are usually more as against a low-price distribution channel such as ordering on the Internet, then the company has to meet the requirements. The channel adds value as much as the product adds value. Companies no longer control what customers are choosing as a buying channel. Now the customers are making that decision.

If efficiency measures or cost savings lower costs to the end customer, then that would be perceived as value by the customer. The customer is both the beneficiary and the judge at the same time. A strategy that emphasizes lean manufacturing, which reduces inventory carrying cost and optimizes production, to meet inventory requirements, is an example of such cases. Reducing lead time is another measure that adds value to end customer. Therefore, how can we eliminate non–value-adding activities? Waste and cycle time reduction is one approach to consider. It is important that suppliers deliver smaller batches and deliver more frequently. Quick customer response to a manufacturer's needs is very important. However, this should not be accomplished by creating waste upstream at the supplier's end. Fast and on-time delivery are value-adding activities. Companies such as Dell computers and American Honda had thrived on such ideas to build their businesses. Dell had learned to build, through cellular manufacturing, computers to order and ship them to individual customers. The choices are simple: either build a huge inventory to respond to customer requests by shipping the next day, which is a very expensive measure, or develop an extremely time efficient value chain where you make things to demand and move things quickly through the system. Obviously, achieving this level in manufacturing is very desirable as it satisfies customer requirements in the most effective manner. The message, inherent in the value chain, is fundamentally determined by the end user (end customer).

Just-in-time (JIT) concepts had been appealing to many businesses for effectiveness implications. Sequencing facilities had been built dedicated to customer products. For example, Wainwright Industries, MO, not only produces stampings for a GM assembly plant, but also operates a JIT warehouse that is dedicated to GM at the same facility. In addition to Wainwright products, the operation handles many parts made by several vendors. Every seven minutes, a truck leaves to make deliveries to the GM plant, with parts arranged in racks in the sequence that they would be needed on the assembly line. In many industries, vendor-managed inventory is becoming a value-adding service. Here, the benefit is greatly reduced inventory and largely reduced administrative transactions such as purchase orders.

Electronic collaboration across supply chains (Yovovich, 1998), or value network, is often viewed as the wave of the future. After companies have optimized their internal business processes, they would be looking into how they can affect value among themselves and their trading partners within that value network. The key in process optimization is that companies should move toward a process model that links functions in the company directly to the customers. The goal is to get a better handle on customer needs and then work backward through every link in the chain from shipping to manufacturing and all the way to raw materials acquisition at the supplier level. The company cannot be internally focused; rather the emphasis is on an external bigger picture view with the customer influencing the process at every step. The goal is not simply to drive down costs, but to be able to respond to changing conditions more quickly and pursue opportunities more aggressively. A company must often make internal changes to pave the way.

A company that is interested in becoming a solution provider rather than a mere component supplier needs to embrace collaboration where its employees get to know the customer processes by actually working at the customer sites. Similarly, customer employees would benefit greatly by spending training time working at the supplier site to learn more about the process. This integration of process learning is crucial to the development of quality systems at both facilities. Through this learning, a supplier might be interested in taking on more components manufacturing and building of subassemblies. Both the supplier and the customer would benefit from added value processes and better quality as well as reduced lead times.

A company is expected to play a part in educating its key suppliers about its business needs. If a company establishes a strategy such as "demand flow," for example, which is a concept in supply chain management, then suppliers should be included in a comprehensive training program that would cover the definite elements required to execute that strategy. Suppliers might be encouraged to move their operations closer to the company's facilities or even create stock rooms or consignment areas within the company's plants. This would benefit closer ties and effectiveness and would truly reflect on the term "partnership." The key to such successful relationships is open communications and mutual respect. This face-to-face relationship surpasses e-mails and telephone calls in bringing partnerships deeper into the fold. For example, American Standard uses White-Rodgers, a division of Emerson Electric in their Trane air conditioning systems. They achieved most of their chain supply partnership through face-to-face conferencing, telephone calls, and faxes. On the other side is Dell computer, which built its manufacturing empire, relying on the same suppliers used by dozens of other competitor companies. They managed their suppliers primarily through cyberspace. Dell's value chain essentially boils down to two websites, one for customers, and one for suppliers. This direct model is key to Dell's marketing strategy and their supply chain simultaneously.

Even value-chain software developers admit that technology is only one piece of the puzzle. The bigger piece is a cultural concern, which is difficult enough when you are tackling the internals of one organization, which nonetheless, becomes greatly pronounced and complex when many different organizations are attempting to work together. For that reason, many companies that are implementing value-chain concepts believe that it is important to reduce your supplier base, identify the companies you work best with, and then look on how you can create better solutions together.

Establishing measurement basis is one important aspect in the manufacturer–supplier relationship. Sharing data is significant; however, discussing the analysis of the data and what it means is more crucial. Typically, the manufacturer holds more power in this partnership, which on occasion results in companies, in their new approaches to business, not asking the supplier to agree to the new way of doing business, but rather demanding it. Manufacturers, however, are sensitive to the fact that suppliers have expertise in what they do, and therefore give their suppliers a chance to describe means of improvement on processes and relationships. Ultimately, the manufacturer, who is the customer, has power (Sellers, 1989). Companies who recognize and understand this sophisticated demand, and work together, will succeed. Being process-driven is not enough; many companies claim that they are process-oriented. However, unless the company finds ways to get closer to its customers and understands their needs, as never before, those processes will have been created in vacuum. "Process owners" of companies need to look from manufacturing to logistics to invoicing to shipping and spend a fair amount of time discussing the issues with the customers, which will bring positive results. For example, through better communications and improved metrics, American Standards moved its fill rate in the wholesale business from 40 percent to an impressive 95 percent. By having someone entirely in charge of the whole process meet with the customers, American Standard was able to work out solutions that are tailored to different situations.

Many executives stress the fact that better forecasting is a key facet of an improved customer–supplier relationship. For example, Wal-Mart Stores and Warner-Lambert collaborated their forecasting effort to improve predictions of sales growth for Listerine mouthwash. Both companies knew that forecasting was a big issue, but they collaborated their effort and brought their information together, which led to faster replenishment, which boosted Wal-Mart's sales of Listerine by $6.5 million. Forecasting discussed in conjunction with marketing plans, promotions, manufacturing capabilities, capacities, and many other factors extending all the way to raw materials, would have achieved the highest synergy for the value chain. Although closer collaboration with customers can lead to better forecasts, extending that kind of communication back to suppliers not only can facilitate timely delivery of goods and services, but also can expand business opportunities.

Many companies today already have at least a manufac-
turing-resource-planning (MRP) system, or a more expansive
enterprise-resource-planning (ERP) system that is either in place
or under development. The biggest challenge is to have the various pieces of the pipeline to connect and talk to one another.
The main problem is an agreement on policies and procedures
that require specific information standards and data protocols.
This becomes even more complicated because of differing pro-
prietary systems offered by numerous vendors. Electronic data
interchange is at the root of the problem. Software companies
such as QAD are offering a message conversion system that lets
companies connect to each other without worrying about incompatible EDI systems. The reliability factor of this conversion and
its extent is not fully known. QAD through e-commerce new
conversion software has eliminated one of the major headaches
by taking responsibility for the syntax and semantics. The issue
of standards was impetus for a computer-industry consortium
called RosettaNet. More than 30 vendors of hardware and software and networking equipment have banded together to set
standards that will let them do a variety of business transactions over the Internet. This IT industry supply chain model is
useful in defining how business processes are conducted among
manufacturers, software companies, distributors, system inte-
grators, and end users. Perhaps more important is what learning this consortium would bring to other industries. Logility,
Inc. offers supply-chain software, which is Web-based for creating a collaborative network for trading partners. This idea
enables companies to connect with their suppliers and customers for planning, forecasting, and replenishment. Manugistics
(acquired by JDA software) offers an e-chain solution to its customers. E-Chain Communities allows companies to share information about their supply chain with their trading partners, and
E-Chain Fulfillment converts selling requirements into supply

needs, meshing inventories, manufacturing capabilities, transport requirements, and material supply.

Del Monte Foods Company is using Data Stream Systems Inc.'s (iProcure) network as its online procurement solution. The network automates e-commerce for MRO procurement, and offers access to maintenance parts and supplies from a list of distributors. Del Monte Foods expects to achieve both operating efficiencies and cost savings by using the purchasing network.

Ingersoll Rand has implemented a massive procurement program using Oracle iSupplier Portal. An integral part of the program is a zero-cost Web-based compliance-labeling program that Ingersoll Rand is offering its global mid-tier suppliers. Using e-barcode 2000, a barcode and printing software, suppliers are able to print compliance labels over the web. Suppliers access IR website, fill out the appropriate information, and then print the label locally through a browser. The program eliminates the need for suppliers to implement on-site software requirements, and enables suppliers to comply with IR's labeling and bar-coding requirements regardless of their own technology level. This capability saves each supplier thousands of dollars annually in meeting bar code and compliance requirements. In addition, the compliance-labeling program reduces IR's processing cost on purchase orders.

Sunoco Inc. implemented Ariba's B2B commerce platform to provide a streamlined, cost-effective private procurement marketplace. Sunoco uses Ariba's buyer system to improve management of direct and indirect goods and services throughout the company.

Cendant member services, Inc., which provides services and direct memberships to shopping clubs, is e-enabling its entire vendor network. The company works with some 400 vendors that drop ship direct to customers. With the availability of electronic options, the company decided to move all its vendors online through SPS commerce purchasing solution. The purchase order files are sent to each of Cendant's suppliers who would send back order acknowledgement, shipping notification, and invoice. In turn, Cendant's systems process the information transmitted by the vendors and use it to perform such tasks as update customer record and web site, generate order correspondence to customer, and cut checks to vendors. In addition, faster, more accurate information from suppliers means that Cendant will be able to be more proactive with customers.

Chain integration aims at the logical solution of shipping directly from the point of origin to the consumer. Managing the pieces that make up the value chain will yield greater value. Elimination of redundancy is high on the agenda for corporate restructuring. Many manufacturers struggle with handling returned products, which often end up discarded, rebuilt, or dismantled into parts. Usually, these steps are costly and time consuming. For example, Great Plains, Inc. offers software that performs the other functions associated with reverse logistics.

For BMW, Customized Transportation Inc. (CTI) adds value by sequencing some 750 stock-keeping units into 10 families of parts prior to final delivery to the assembly plant based on production signals from the BMW inventory management system. CTI delivers the material to the production line within a two-hour window.

Not everyone likes the idea of using the Internet to cut huge chunks of the supply chain. For example, Home Depot Inc., observes Web-based sales by its suppliers as a threat to sales of products in its vast store network. Home Depot warned its suppliers about competitive threats if they offered to sell their products over the web. Home Depot does not mainly sell goods over the Internet, but are planning to expand this effort.

VIT software began marketing SeeChain, a set of supply-chain-performance applications. The metrics software works with various supply-chain systems such as i2, Manugistics, Oracle, and SAP, and measures results in the form of key performance indicators. Managers need data to work out intuitive solutions that allow them to find the root cause of a problem and get on with fixing it. These measurements allow companies to synchronize supply chain strategies with long-term business initiatives. Seechain measures the accuracy of demand forecasts and production plans, as well as on-time delivery and customer-service levels. It also monitors raw materials and finished goods.

Another example is VIP software, which is designed to help companies identify and improve supply chain challenges such as customer and vendor quality levels, transaction price management, order-fulfillment cycle time, and fill rates.

The supply chain connects a longer channel starting with raw materials and ending with final products that are carried to final buyers. On the other hand, marketing channels connect the marketer to the target buyers. The supply chain represents a value delivery system, of which each company captures a certain percentage of the total value generated by the chain. Acquisitions and divestitures are a reflection of whether a company has chosen to capture a higher percentage of the supply chain value by becoming more vertically integrated or moved downstream to capture cost reductions or efficiency depending on the particular chain link that fits with the overall company strategy.

The value chain identifies strategic relevant activities that create value. The primary activities represent the sequence of bringing materials into the business (inbound logistics), converting them into final products, shipping out those final products (outbound logistics), marketing them, and servicing them. The company needs to examine its costs and performance in each value-adding activity and always look for continuous improvement. These data should be benchmarked against competitors' performance to the extent that the company activities can achieve a competitive advantage. A firm's success depends not only on how well each department performs its work, but also on how well the various departmental activities are coordinated. To ensure that departments are not building walls (silos) that slow down the delivery of quality customer service, many companies have elected to focus on core business processes that are managed by cross-functional teams, such that the product would smoothly move from R&D to production. Inventory levels are managed to provide adequate supplies at the right cost. Acquiring customers and retaining them is of the highest priority. All activities pertaining to on-time delivery of goods to satisfy a customer order are of utmost importance. The customer must be able to reach resources in the company and should be able to receive quick and satisfactory service and timely resolution of problems.

TQM

At the heart of the value chain are customers (Gitomer, 1998) that expect high product and service quality from the vendor. Improving this quality level is viewed as a top priority. Most customers will no longer accept or tolerate average quality. Companies have to adopt TQM to remain in the race and sustain a competitive position. TQM is an organizational approach to put the company on a path of continuous improvement, by improving the quality of all the organization's processes, products, and services.

The Malcolm Baldrige Quality award criteria consist of seven measures: ustomer focus and satisfaction, quality and operational results, management of process quality, human resource development, strategic quality planning, information analysis and management, and executive leadership. ISO 9000 is generally accepted as the international standard for documenting quality. It provides a framework for showing customers how quality systems in a particular business are documented with respect to product testing, employee training, record keeping, and deviation analysis. Earning ISO 9000 certification involves a quality audit from a registered assessor.

Included in the marketing plan must be a provision to participate in formulating strategies and policies designed to help the company achieve total quality excellence. Marketing activities of market research, sales training, advertising, or customer service must be performed to high standards similar to quality demands on product manufacturing, delivering, and servicing.

Marketers play several roles in helping their companies define and deliver high-quality goods to target customers. They communicate customers' expectations to product designers. They should make sure that customer orders are filled correctly on time and that he/she receives the right instructions and technical assistance to use the product. They remain in touch with the customer to ensure his/her satisfaction. They should follow up on product improvement programs. The marketing group should be the internal voice of the customer striving to give the customer the best possible solution.

To improve a company's value chain as a means to reduce cycle time, cut costs, and improve order-to-deliver time for customers, the right people and the right systems must be put in place to achieve the desired goal. A good value chain is a series of players who play together as a team, each adding some component of value, such as faster assembly, more accurate information, and better customer response to the overall process. For many manufacturers, the key elements in the plan are an internal information backbone and multiple external connections to suppliers, dealers, and customers.

9

Freestyle and Movement

The pace of technological change results in ever-shorter product life cycles and a continuous search for enhanced efficiency, which is characterized by a fierce competition for market share. To achieve these goals, firms must use information technology (IT) with foresightedness to redesign business processes, improve supply chain management, and increase the value provided to the customer. This competitive environment provides an exceptional laboratory for evaluating how companies use IT to create business value. The goal of "enhanced efficiency" requires the use of IT to achieve a greater market share. In addition, IT systems are intrinsic to improve users' performance, and to make the tools of the organization user friendly so that they can be used by individuals to maximize speed of information and efficiency, reduce material loss, and boost productivity as a result of faster decision making. This will provide for the competitive edge.

Intensifying global competition and increasingly sophisticated consumer preferences require companies to respond quickly and effectively to market opportunities. To accomplish these goals, managers need timely and comprehensive information to make good marketing, production, and distribution decisions. As Michael E. Porter, the leading authority on competitive strategy from Harvard Business School, and coauthor, Victor E. Millar, noted in the 1985 edition of *Harvard Business Review*, "The information revolution is changing the nature of business and *can* create competitive advantages for those managers who understand its effects." Questions remain, however, about how firms should use IT to gain this value.

Michael Hammer, a former professor of computer science at the Massachusetts Institute of Technology (MIT), published an article in 1990 in the *Harvard Business Review*, in which he advocated the use of IT to make radical changes in business processes: "We should 'reengineer' our businesses: use the power of modern information technology to radically redesign our business processes in order to achieve dramatic improvements in their performance." Many firms followed his advice; however, Hammer himself admits that the results of these efforts were mixed and stresses the importance of IT to achieve "information integration," but he also points out that "true information integration won't happen without major changes in management approaches and organizational structure."

Firms use IT to deliver value to their customers, to keep their current customers, and gain new ones. Michael Porter explains, "A company must deliver greater value to its customers or create comparable value at a lower cost, or do both." Any differences in cost, price, or quality of products derive from the execution of business activities that make up the firm's business processes. While these objectives are clearly desirable, implementing them can be a challenge. How should management combine reengineering or business process redesign with use of IT in a specific organizational culture? What are the cause and effect relationships? What actions must the firm's management take to derive value from their IT and business process redesign efforts? How can they measure the results? Figure 9.1 shows the steps in the Internal Business Process.

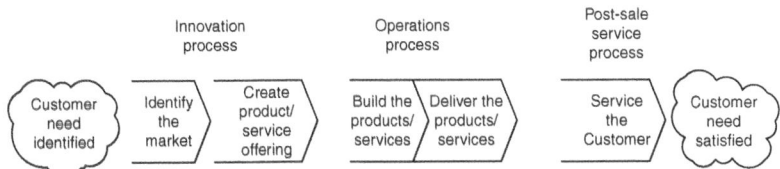

Figure 9.1 Internal Business Process Steps.

IT Strategic Impact

Monitoring technology investments vary widely. As technology cost, complexity, and consequences grow, managers need a framework to develop IT policies that fit the companies they oversee. Oversight for IT activities is dangerous; it puts the firm at risk in the same way that failing to audit its books would.

Leaders consider it their job to bring creative talent back the next morning after each and every day at work. Creativity can't be shoehorned between the hours of nine-to-five. Muses don't always show up on time for appointments. It's important to make sure people throughout the organization hear customers' voices loud, clear, and unfiltered—so they're as unambiguous as a stock quote. Table 9.1 compares impact of offensive against defensive IT strategies.

Questions

- Has the strategic importance of our IT changed?
- What are our current and potential competitors doing in the area of IT?
- Are we following best practices in asset management?
- Is the company getting adequate ROI from information resources?
- Do we have the appropriate IT infrastructure and applications to exploit the development of our intellectual assets?
- Has anything changed in disaster recovery and security that will affect our business continuity planning?

Table 9.1 IT Strategic Impact

Defensive	Offensive
1. Factory mode <ul><li>If systems fail for a minute or more, there is an immediate loss of business</li><li>Decrease in response time beyond one second has serious consequences for both internal and external users</li><li>Most core business activities are online</li><li>Systems work is mostly maintenance</li><li>Systems work provides little strategic differentiation or dramatic cost reduction</li><li>Need for reliable, but not necessarily new IT</li></ul>	**1. Strategic mode** <ul><li>If systems fail for a minute or more, there is an immediate loss of business</li><li>Decrease in response time beyond one second has serious consequences for both internal and external users</li><li>New systems promise major process and service transformations</li><li>New systems promise major cost reductions</li><li>New systems will close significant cost, service, or process performance gap with competitors</li><li>Need for both reliable and new IT</li></ul>
2. Support mode <ul><li>Even with repeated service interruptions of up to 12 hours, there are no serious consequences</li><li>User response time can take up to five seconds with online transactions</li><li>Internal systems are almost invisible to suppliers and customers. There is little need for extranet capability</li><li>Company can quickly revert to manual procedures for 80% of value transactions</li><li>Systems work is mostly maintenance</li><li>Less dependent on both reliable or new IT</li></ul>	**2. Turnaround mode** <ul><li>New systems promise major process and service transformations</li><li>New systems promise major cost reductions</li><li>New systems will close significant cost, service, or process performance gap with competitors</li><li>IT constitutes more than 50% of capital spending</li><li>IT makes up more than 15% of total corporate expenses</li><li>Need more new IT than just reliable IT</li></ul>

- Do we have management practices in place that will prevent our hardware, software, and legacy applications from becoming obsolete?
- Do we have adequate protection against denial of service and hackers?
- Are there fast-response processes in place in the event of an attack?
- Do we have management processes in place to ensure 24/7 service levels, including tested backup?
- Are we protected against possible intellectual property-infringement lawsuits?
- Are there any possible IT-based surprises lurking out there?
- Are our strategic IT development plans proceeding as required?
- Is our application portfolio sufficient to deal with a competitive threat or to meet a potential opportunity?
- Do we have processes in place that will enable us to discover and execute any strategic IT opportunities?
- Do we have processes in place to guard against IT risk?
- Do we regularly benchmark to maintain our competitive cost structure?

It is not an exaggeration to assert that rapid and relentless economic Darwinism has prevailed, and continues to prevail, in industry. Industry participants confront aggressive pricing practices, continually changing customer demand patterns, growing competition from well-capitalized high technology and consumer electronics companies, and rapid technological development carried out in the midst of legal battles over intellectual property rights. Figure 9.2 reflects on the sales order fulfillment process.

Survival in the IT industry requires that firms continuously reevaluate and improve their business processes, especially their value chains. ERP software, such as SAP AG's R/3, or Oracle is used to implement changes in business processes. Leveraging this technology enables companies to restructure resources, gain efficiencies, improve market reach, and implement corporate

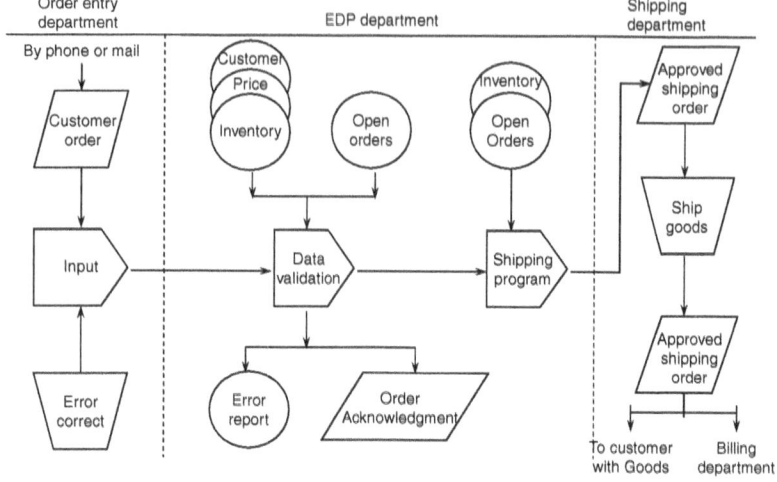

Figure 9.2   Sales Order Fulfillment.

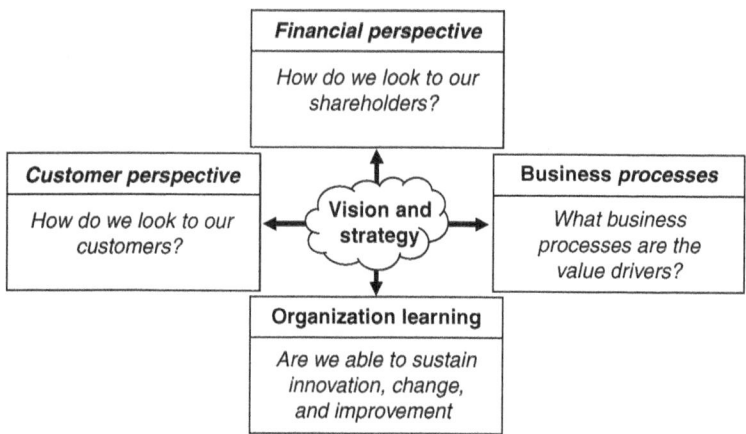

Figure 9.3   Business Balanced Scorecard's Four Pillars.

strategies more effectively. Figure 9.3 emphasizes the significance of relationships between financial perspective, customer
relations, business processes, and learning strategies within a
firm overall strategy in support of its mission.

The Effects of Build-to-order

Under a build-to-order (BTO) process model, the manufacturer begins to assemble products only after an order has been placed. Using BTO, Dell personal computers averaged less than ten days to sell its inventory. Dell's efficient BTO model gave competition a target for its manufacturing and distribution processes. Competition had relied on "build-to-forecast," an inherently more efficient manufacturing process characterized by large production runs and low unit costs. In the PC industry, however, any unsold product has a very short shelf life. New products are introduced constantly and product lines often have only a life of a few months. Competition had to deal with obsolete products in both its own inventory and the inventory held by its retail dealers and resellers. Obsolescent inventory—with lowered prices—competed with new products. In addition, competition was faced with substantial product returns each time a new product was introduced. The extra handling and disposition were wasteful and costly.

Intense price competition and other factors have caused several PC manufacturers to lose market share and then regain it as they brought out competitive models that sold for less, except for the premium models such as Apple. Their ability to price their products without a retailer markup, however, allowed them to market high performance systems for well under 2000 dollars, and this contributed to their strength in the consumer marketplace.

Dell continued its success in the commercial (business) marketplace as a leading direct marketer of computer systems. Dell's ability to leverage IT fueled its growth in an industry characterized by declining prices. Dell maintains lower costs by bypassing distributors and other resellers. Dell was the first to use a BTO methodology to manufacture and distribute computers according to specific customer orders. They have focused their organization and their use of IT to implement their business strategy: to minimize inventories and more effectively manage their supply chain. In fact, Dell's factory converts customer orders into desktop PCs ready for delivery in an average of eight hours.

In the PC business, sagacious use of enterprise-level IT is essential to implement business strategies and be fully competitive. The following excerpt from Dell's 10K report, although addressing only the customer awareness aspect, highlights the importance of IT in implementing business strategies. Great emphasis is placed on customer service, the understanding of market trends, and the use of enterprise software that provides the necessary information.

> Dell's information systems enable the company to track each unit sold from the initial sales contacts, through the manufacturing process to post-sales service and support. Dell is able to track key information about many of its customers and target marketing activities specifically to particular types of customers by using its database to assess purchasing trends, advertising effectiveness, customer, and product groupings. This database, unique to Dell's direct model, allows the Company to gauge customer satisfaction issues and also provides the opportunity to test new propositions in the marketplace prior to product or service introductions.

Good business practice demanded a cross-functional process. Designers and engineers needed market information on both market requirements (e.g., interoperability of systems components, reducing cost of ownership, typical uses, and configuration preferences), and on competitors' innovations. Also needed were data from suppliers and manufacturing information to design-for-manufacturability. A "best practice" team approach dictated that the marketing members of the team specify the product requirements and the manufacturing members set the production constraints.

Manufacturing and Distribution Processes

Competition needed to improve its inventory management. BTO should eliminate these problems by reducing inventory levels. BTO, however, requires a much higher level of supply chain integration and management: Physical inventory must be replaced with information. Suppliers must know the delivery requirements of their customer. If the flow of products were to be delayed, the customer would not have the parts and subassemblies necessary to assemble complete, and the BTO process would break down.

Pricing Process

Pricing objectives are considered ambitious, if owner wants to set the prices for the market. At the same time, if he also wants pricing to create value for his customers in ways that will differentiate his products. In a highly competitive industry, achieving these pricing goals requires detailed and timely sales information. An agile company that can adjust to changes in the volatile marketplace is the one that succeeds. In the retail channel, companies need sales information on a daily basis to price its products correctly without compromising its profit margins. In the reseller channel, companies need more timely information about its end customers' requirements so that it could develop solutions that would add more value than competitors' products at a lower total cost of ownership.

One aspect of pricing is product quality, that is, assessing whether the product meets all of the customer's requirements. A competitor's success in the major corporate market hinges on its ability to deliver complete enterprise-wide solutions. Its customers typically seek to avoid dealing with multiple vendors, and they do not want to struggle to integrate potentially incompatible products. They want suppliers to provide complete solutions and then price the products appropriately. Consistent with these objectives, to add the necessary expertise and product lines, competitors integrate vertically and horizontally and form alliances with major vendors.

Ultimately, the performance of any business process depends on both the abilities and knowledge of the people who perform that process, their incentives, and the management's practices. Reengineering efforts align decision making with business process operations. Consequently, management becomes both cross-functional and cross-process in scope, with decision making assigned to "put the decision point where the work is performed and build control into the process," says Hammer.

The success of any organizational change depends on the culture at the process level, the degree of centralization of common processes, and the nature of information sharing. Unless the organization is committed to operational excellence, there is little hope of achieving quality class performance, and Hammer advises companies to "organize around outcomes."

Restructuring an organization around new business processes requires an enterprise information system that can capture and integrate information across the entire value chain. As an organization seeks to assign decision rights at the process level, the timeliness and accuracy of the decisions become dependent on access to necessary information. Therefore, successful implementation of strategy depends critically on the ability to deliver information in a timely, reliable, and usable manner. Improvements in the role of information, and integrated enterprise-wide operations are key to support and measure process performance. To obtain the required technology, competitors tap both their own resources and those of major partners. The solutions that are developed for largest corporate customers are also applied within.

As a part of their enterprise system, On-Line allows channel members to configure, price, and order products online. Online system is live and interactive; for example, Amazon website allows the customer to place orders and receive confirmation immediately. It also builds tracking into order processing, status, and shipping information. On-Line's planned integration is intended to create links spanning the entire value chain, from suppliers to customers. Sales force automation and e-commerce engines are provided. Figure 9.4 depicts estimation of the information flows that these systems should achieve. Competitors eventually will be able to match orders with manufacturing and distribution in real time, allowing them to adjust manufacturing plans and schedules every few hours at plants, and at distribution centers globally.

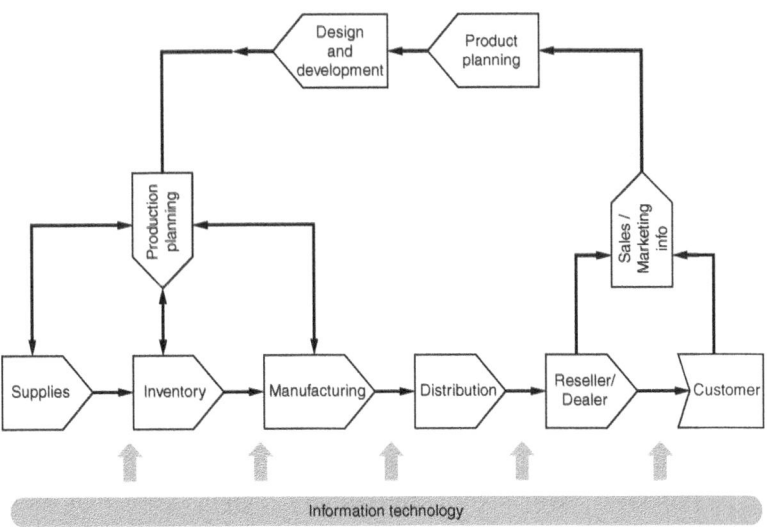

Figure 9.4   IT Impact on the Value Chain.

Optimized Distribution Model (ODM)

The initial phase of ODM is BTO. The second phase is Configure-to-Order (CTO), where competitors will configure products to customer specification and deliver to resellers to fulfill the order. The third phase is the Channel Configuration Program (CCP), where competitors deliver configurable products (partially assembled products) to resellers who will then customize those products to meet specific customer requirements. Figure 9.4 shows IT impact on the value chain.

IT architecture is designed to gather information on worldwide demand and customer preferences, and respond accordingly. This enterprise-wide system will allow competitors to:

1. Monitor supply and demand factors around the world on a daily basis, and better understand customer requirements. Senior management sees—in real time—a global representation of the market and can respond promptly to market changes. Implementing ODM to reduce inventory levels and improve productivity can shift resources rapidly to respond to changes anywhere in the world, making planning processes much more agile. Automatically make necessary foreign currency translations and provide the necessary currency information to reduce risk.

2. Make team members more aware of their roles and responsibilities—and how their actions affect others. For example, marketing people can share information with members of the design and manufacturing team, resulting in products that are more consistent with customer preferences. Companies will then be able to respond rapidly to any competitive pressures. Company shares information across its supply chain. A leaner, more focused organization is created given the e-commerce capabilities, improved inventory management, and automated processes such as the "configurator" applications that allow customers to configure, price, and order products. By sharing information electronically with suppliers, competitors

can effectively outsource many of their component assembly processes.

How do we *measure* the payoff from investment in IT? The literature suggests that the payoff from IT should be evaluated in terms of the business objectives that it supports. Technology must be aligned with the core competencies of the company to deliver true value. Companies address the impact of technology improvements in both the efficiency and effectiveness of the affected business processes. Most important, should consider not only past results but also implied future benefits (e.g., goodwill).

Executive management needs performance measurements that indicate the extent to which the company is achieving its strategic objectives. While they are used extensively, traditional financial accounting measurements do not reveal adequately the benefits of investing in information technologies. Financial accounting measurements do inform management of historical outcomes but do not indicate why those results were achieved or what management must do to improve future results. Excessive reliance on financial accounting performance measurements is inadequate at best, and can be very misleading, due to the following limitations:

1. Financial accounting provides very little indication of why results were (or were not) achieved or how to improve the firm's strategy.
2. Only ill-defined linkages are revealed between the effectiveness and/or efficiency of business processes and financial results.
3. Long-term assets are reported at historical cost, which may be unrelated to current value.
4. Management treats economic events subjectively by selecting among feasible accounting methods.

Cause and effect linkages are identified by mapping the execution of daily activities to eventual results. Consistent with this theme, performance measurements are considered from four perspectives:

1. Learning and growth for the organization and its members: The focus is on the firm's employees, their skills, satisfaction, motivation, innovation, and productivity. These attributes precondition process improvements, customer satisfaction, and ultimately financial success.
2. Operation of internal business processes: The focus is on optimizing costs, quality, throughput, and time attributes of each process.
3. Satisfaction of customers: The focus is on customer satisfaction and the resulting changes in market share, new customer acquisition, customer retention, and customer profitability.
4. Financial results: Based on the above three perspectives, the focus is on outcome measures of revenue growth, cost reduction, and asset utilization. Clearly, innovative new products that are accepted enthusiastically by the market and are produced efficiently will result in superior financial performance.

The first three perspectives yield sets of performance measurements that are directly implied by the firm's strategic objectives. However, corporate stakeholders ultimately want to see results in a language they understand—financial results. Both financial and non-financial performance measurements are essential in performance analysis. Measurements are also identified as being either leading or lagging indicators. Leading measurements motivate future action to improve the firm's business processes. The leading indicators are linked to future results; in contrast, the lagging measurements represent the firm's *effectiveness* in achieving its objectives. Since the lagging measurements document past results, they may also be studied to achieve more efficient use of the firm's resources. Figure 9.5 shows Balanced scorecard representation of causes and effects (linkages) between financial, customer, business, and training (learning) strategies.

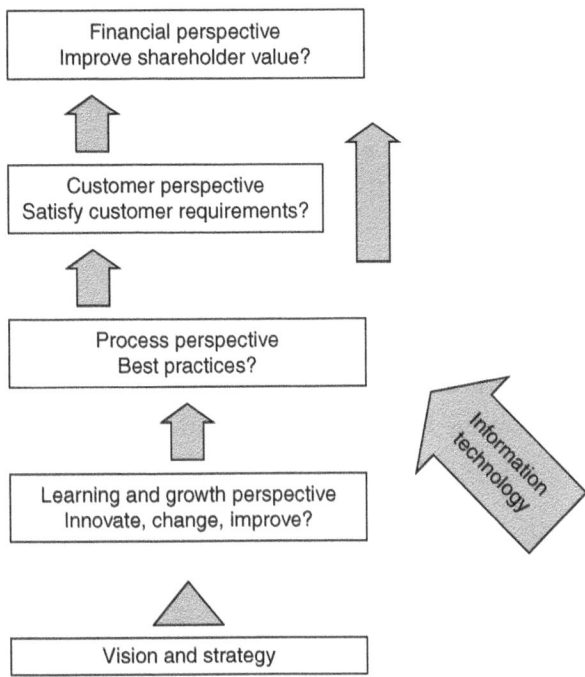

Figure 9.5   Balanced Scorecard Representation of Causes and Effects.

Firms should choose the market and customer segments the business unit intends to serve, identify critical business processes that must deliver value to those customers, and select the individual and organizational capabilities that are required to meet these objectives. Ultimately, a company must deliver value to its customers, value as a function of product attributes (e.g., functionality, quality, price, and timeliness), company image, and customer relationships. Market share provides one important measure of customer satisfaction; it reflects marketplace acceptance of the price and performance of products. It also clearly indicates the effect of the effort that a company has made to create a positive image and develop relationships with its customers.

Companies compete in a dynamic marketplace. Customers' requirements change. Relationships can be short-lived. Therefore, retaining a customer can be difficult. Competitors bet that they can create and sustain value by expanding product lines and increasing their service capabilities, combining the resources to deliver the best solutions and innovative products and technologies, all backed by global services and support. First, during the first innovation cycle, products are designed and developed. Then, during the operations cycle, products are made, marketed, and serviced. The performance of these two cycles creates value for the customer and for the business itself. Suitable use of IT can profoundly improve these cycles.

Innovation Cycle

The innovation process, the long wave of value creation, is for many companies a more powerful driver of future financial performance than the short-term operating cycle. For competitors, the innovation cycle is focused on speed. Kirkpatrick and Curry in 1996 stated that "competitors thrive on speed—speedy revenue growth, speedy market share gains, speed in entering new business, and speed in manufacturing. The environment is changing, and you'd better be innovative—not just in your products but in every part of your business."

Product innovation focuses on specific market objectives and price points, reducing time to market, and designing products to match customer requirements while considering component availability. For example, PCs quickly captured almost 40 percent of the under-one-thousand dollar retail market in 1997, attracting buyers that had previously been unable to afford PCs. Most importantly, competitors were able to design and develop this product at a price point that allowed them to maintain their gross profit margin. Reengineering efforts reduced the time to market of new products. These new products empha-size enhanced functionality, or price advantages, which in turn improve customer satisfaction and product image.

Operations Cycle

The operations cycle encompasses sourcing parts and compo-nents, manufacturing, configuring, marketing, distributing, and servicing products after the sale. Reengineering projects typically include expansion of a company's distribution center, the implementation of a new inventory tracking system, and an overhaul of the company's information management system.

Ongoing reengineering efforts continue to emphasize process efficiency. The reengineering effort is a long effort. It requires changing business processes first and then information systems to support the new business process. "The objectives for any cost savings that would result should not end up on the bot-tom line. They need to flow back into prices being more com-petitive, pushing market share...to get the inefficiency out and re-funnel the money into those things that really create success and customer satisfaction" (Farre, 1997).

Competitors rely heavily on enterprise-level IT to achieve reengineering gains. These innovations allow competitors to achieve process efficiencies, including the following:

- Linking orders electronically with production and suppliers, improving cycle time; facilitating just-in-time manufacturing, and making production status information available so that cus-tomers can track their own orders.
- Sharing information with suppliers allows them to anticipate changes in demand and improve their efficiency, thereby reduc-ing costs of supplies and improving on-time delivery.
- Exchanging information on parts and component availability with suppliers allows products to be configured with the most

economical and readily available components, reducing costs and improving cycle time.

- Integrating orders with ERP software such as SAP, or Oracle financial management and production planning modules, reducing time and cost of orders processing for both resellers and other customers.
- Capturing customer information after a sale to provide individualized service as well as additional marketing based on information about the specific products and configurations ordered by each customer.

These process efficiencies would not have been possible without the large investment in IT. In addition to creating the systems, employees must take on the daunting task of learning the new systems and continually improving them over time.

Learning and Growth Objectives

A company cannot innovate or operate well without creating long-term learning and growth. Organizational learning and growth come from three principal sources: people, systems, and organizational procedures.

Competitors, for example, use alliances with value-added resellers (VAR) to extend their own capabilities to meet customer requirements and obtain information on customer needs and preferences. For example, large business customers are accustomed to the kind of handholding for which IBM is famous. The VARs provide this capability for competitors such that they get to play in the big-iron business without incurring the costs of running their own business services.

Partnerships allow competitors to focus on core competencies. For example, if management determined that product warranty repairs and service is not a core competency, so it contracts with a vendor as its worldwide service provider. Partnerships also open new markets and create synergistic demand for both partners' products: for example, the partnership with Apple and AT &T, where AT&T promotes Apple's wireless products. E-commerce systems are designed to achieve efficient exchange of information to and from its partners. Where capabilities are particularly important to strategic objectives, making partnerships less desirable, competitors use financial strength to acquire them. These acquisitions provide expertise in networking and transaction-intensive systems needed for the large business market.

Sustainable growth strategy, which emphasizes BTO manufacturing, multichannel distribution, pricing, promotion, and customer service, is built for the longer term. To achieve growth, any company needs to keep current customers and acquire new ones—it must create customer satisfaction. The drivers of customer satisfaction are: price, brand image, and service.

Price

One of the most important drivers of customer satisfaction is price. Reductions in prices should be accompanied by reductions in costs. Competitors reduce costs by achieving process efficiency. Competitors engaged in a series of process reengineering efforts that reduced cycle times, increased inventory turnover, and reduced the cost of raw materials. These efficiencies allowed competitors to reduce prices as much as 15 percent per annum, thereby driving customer satisfaction.

Brand Image

In addition to aggressive advertising and promotional programs, competitors reinforced brand image by improving the functionality of products and scope of product line. This is where the innovation cycle and the speed with which innovations occur are most involved. By reengineering product innovation processes, competitors were able to reduce time to market and enhance product functionality while designing products that were less costly to manufacture. Product innovation allowed them to meet changing customer requirements and derive customer satisfaction.

Service

Achieving higher process level improvements to enhance customer satisfaction requires organizational learning and growth. Management has to become very knowledgeable about customer requirements. It should constantly monitor and improve processes to keep costs down. The enterprise-wide systems feed business intelligence data to management with information that should allow them to make better decisions and improve process performance, which in turn would bring in customer satisfaction.

Some competitors perceived the consolidation of facilities and business processes was more important than process innovation in the short run. They could not focus on faster cycle times and lower inventory levels until it was decided which products would be kept, which facilities would remain, and how workforces would be integrated. The competition for management attention may have limited ability to monitor sales and balance inventory levels. Alternatively, the desire to meet growth objectives unduly influenced actions. In either case, instead of the targeted level of shorter weeks-inventory in the channel, there were longer weeks-inventory in the channel, which influenced delivery negatively.

Competitors are forced to take drastic action to eliminate excess inventory before the products become obsolete. They cut prices and begin aggressive marketing campaigns. They slow down assembly lines for few weeks to reduce inventory and they disrupt internal business processes, thus delaying new product introductions, and actually cause some shortages. In these cases, competitors lose ground to companies using BTO production.

Better information drives learning and growth and enables more efficient business processes. Better information is necessary if competitors are to understand and meet customers' constantly changing requirements. Managers and employees, suppliers, and VARs need enterprise-wide access to that information to coordinate their activities across the value chain and continuously improve company business processes.

The causal linkage among the various balanced scorecard perspectives drives the resulting financial measures and market share results. Competitors improved sales volumes that resulted from delivering value, increasing customer service, innovating new products, and reducing time-to-market. The growing sales volume more than offset decreasing prices to generate higher revenue. Improved cycle times and decreasing costs enabled competitors to operate more efficiently, which resulted in higher net income levels and higher revenue.

As Robert S. Kaplan, the Marvin Bower Professor of Leadership Development, Emeritus at the Harvard Business School, and David P. Norton, president of Renaissance Solutions Inc., noted in 1996, "Financial measures are inadequate for guiding and evaluating organizations' trajectories through competitive environments. They are lagging indicators that fail to capture much of the value that has been created or destroyed by managers' actions." Therefore, emphasizing leading indicators, such as pricing innovations, strategic partnerships, and process reengineering efforts, assess the contribution of IT to companies' economic success.

Balanced scorecard analysis of competitors indicates that, rather than a single factor, it is the well-managed combination of factors, facilitated by access to—and prudent use—of information, that leads to good performance. For example,

- Business strategy—a clearly defined and communicated business strategy is important. There is a difference, however, between strategy formulation and strategy implementation. Competitors formed strategies, and immediately identified the processes that were necessary to achieve strategic objectives. They also used these strategies as a basis for prioritizing IT investments.
- Process efficiency—a number of firms succeeded with reengineering or total quality management efforts. However, even Michael Hammer admitted that less than one-third of reengineering efforts succeeds (Slavin, 1994). Competitors have reengineered several times in a successful search for greater efficiency and/or effectiveness.
- IT—many firms implement ERP systems, as is indicated by the impressive growth of ERP vendors such as SAP AG, PeopleSoft, Baan Macula, and Oracle. Often firms use such comprehensive software applications as a means to achieve reengineering, but the success of the IT investment is then inextricably linked to the success of the reengineering effort. If either the system implementation or the reengineering fails—both of which are risky—firms face large write-offs.
- Alliances—alliances provide the leverage for firms to extend their own resources to achieve growth and reduce costs. Competitors leveraged relationships with suppliers to establish strong footholds in both the consumer and corporate market. They work with resellers to leverage sales and support resources. In addition, they use size to obtain favorable prices and to ensure availability of components. To manage these important relationships along value chain, competitors use IT extensively—the Total Order Planning System is a prominent example.
- Skilled and motivated workforce—it is obviously the workforce—from the CEO down—which determines how well a firm innovates and operates. Competitors emphasized a culture that rewards both innovation and efficiency (Kirkpatrick and Curry, 1996; Nee, 1998).

Thus, a synergistic combination of factors has driven competitors' success. Processes create innovative products and address customer requirements. Process efficiencies allow lower product prices and improve the return on resources applied. Of course, the better customer requirements are met, the greater the customer satisfaction and the larger the market share. Nevertheless, the "bottom line" is a firm's profitability. All the other actions must be taken with that long-term financial result in mind. Competitors focus on bottom line results, but also understand the performance drivers of those results. Competitors are facing the challenge of mergers between companies, combining their resources, and linking IT systems. The question remains whether the new company can achieve the same level of performance along all the balanced scorecard perspectives.

Jim Manzi, former CEO of Lotus Development, says "the key to productivity lies not in the computers themselves but in how they are used. 'Use,' in this instance, refers to how information technology fits into the overall structure of the organization and how it helps achieve organizational goals. The potential of information technology is realized only when that technology is integrated into the strategic vision of the organization and when it is used to redefine job structures, processes and lines of authority."

10

Momentum and Continuity

According to the Stockdale paradox (prisoner dreaming of a better life): Confronting the brutal facts of current difficulties and continuing to believe in prevailing at the end is a measure of the ability to persevere (perseverance strength).

Things do not happen overnight—rather, we need to relentlessly push a giant flywheel in one direction until momentum kicks in (Collins, 2001). Keep the momentum and do not lurch back and forth with radical change programs, reactionary moves, and restructuring, which will affect progress and hinder ultimate goals. Focus the effort on three main concepts: (1) core competence; (2) economics; and (3) igniting passion in people— *Eliminate everything else that does not fit*. Watch out for technology bandwagon. Apply carefully selected technologies that will turbocharge the business.

Momentum transfer is key to initiatives being followed vigorously. Efforts applied consistently in the same direction makes big things move forward. Doing many small things as part of a step-by-step, systematic process creates substantial results.

Every physical process has hurdles (activation energy) and a threshold. It is through the accumulation of knowledge and know-how (expertise) that a breakthrough to pass threshold is accomplished.

Transformations usually happen upon alignment of key steps in the process. The faster we organize activities and define objectives the faster these transformations will happen.

Common denominators will allow building enough momentum to create transformation. Deliberate change will organize thought and activities to make things happen. It is an evolutionary process. Little by little all of them stacked together will emit the steady glow of success rather than a flash of light. The following example about Eli Lilly & Co. demonstrates the concept of transformation methodology for growth.

Eli Lilly

Persuasive evidence to win support over competitive opportunities, Colonel Lilly sought to make medicines according to recognized scientific criteria: precise formulation, accurate compounding, standardization, full disclosure of ingredients, and honest claims. Forces threatening to hold down prices were intensifying competition from generic drugs introduced after their patent expired. The profit secured from new drugs, even more than the past, was a function of how long firms fully harvested their patents. Speed to market, manufacturing ramp-up could be critical to extending that period. However, companies charge higher prices during initial years of their patents, when they face little competition. The sophisticated and complex manufacturing processes had increased the minimum efficient scale of a new bulk active ingredient patent. To keep this process in perspective, Lilly, among others, needed to recoup costs of R&D and clinical trials that spread over 10 to 15 years for the commercial application of a pharmaceutical active ingredient (API). Clinical trials run in three phases depending on each phase success before an API / drug can be moved to commercialization under a patent application. All these processes emphasized momentum sustainability to ensure continuity of these type of operations.

Phase I trials tested whether the drug was safe for humans at recommended dosage levels. Phase II attempted to demonstrate whether the drug actually worked for the claimed application. Phase III set of clinical trials, typically the longest and most expensive, simultaneously tested safety and efficacy of the drug more thoroughly and in larger patient population. At the end of a successful phase III, the company would file for a new drug application (NDA) with the food and drug administration (FDA).

Initiatives

The following are key initiatives in transformation methodology for growth:

1. Remain focused on products / markets where company has core competencies and competitive advantages.
2. Vertically integrate all strategic operations. Outsource all other non-strategic activities.
3. Acquire and horizontally integrate other companies that would fit company, and which are compatible and complementary to implementing company strategic objectives.
4. Keep and focus products / services that can be number one or two in market share within three years. Divest others. Focus on value-adding chain activities only.
5. Gear all process improvements towards world-class (excellence) standards and ensure signature of quality systems.
6. Invest in knowledge management systems including ERP. Fortify learning and growth by promoting a learning culture.

Elements of Transformation Methodology for Growth

Strategy executions, knowledge management, and financial strategies such as hedging and money exchange are lead factors for growth for multinational corporations' global operations. The following will highlight interests in these matters for catapulting a business into higher levels of performance.

Strategy Execution

A lack of vision is detrimental to strategy; however, the lack of execution of strategy is fatal. According to Compaq chairman Benjamin Rosen, "The change will not be in our fundamental strategy—we think that strategy is sound—but in execution." "Our plans are to speed up decision-making and make the company more efficient."

It is bad execution, as simple as that: not getting things done, being indecisive, not delivering on commitments. Sometimes CEOs adopt a strategy so flawed that it is doomed, or they refuse to confront reality in their market.

The worldwide revolution of free markets, open economies, and lowered trade barriers and the advent of e-commerce have made virtually every business far more brutally competitive. The frantic spread of information through technology is making customers everywhere more powerful and pushing toward global commodities markets.

CEO failures are pronounced by failure to put the right people in the right jobs, and the related failure to fix people problems in a timely manner. This is a major problem and failure of emotional strength. Many inexperienced people in jobs have moved into higher jobs with their high-level execution abilities untested.

Lou Gerstner of IBM posits, "The last thing IBM needs right now is a vision." He focused on execution, decisiveness, simplifying the organization for speed, and breaking the gridlock. The best CEOs are interested in people. They then grow them into positions and jobs of increasing complexity. "People first—strategy second." Effective CEOs use processes to drive decisions, not delay them. They start by focusing on initiatives that are clear, specific, and few. They do not launch a new one until those in progress are embedded in the company culture. They avoid jargon such as vision statement, quality imitative, empowerment, leadership, but focus on execution.

A trait of a successful CEO is to grab a pen and write exactly what is supposed to be done by whom and when. He/she will go over the tasks with everyone before the meeting closes. He/she will probably follow up by sending a reminder to each one. Failure in process is usually due to ignoring commitments. Commitments are everything. Kodak had created a remarkably aggressive plan to remake itself as a digital imaging company. "Plausible strategy–no execution." They lacked a charge out of pushing to make things happen. Successful CEOs do not do what they want; they do what must be done, what reality demands, what markets dictate. They face market realities.

Obsession with strategy and vision can feed the mistaken belief that developing the right strategy exactly will enable a company to skyrocket beyond its competitors. Michael Dell believed that his strategy is obvious to competition. He affirmed that his teams execute the strategy. It is all about knowledge and execution. Toyota offers tours of its operations; they believe that visitors will not figure out the real advantage of how they execute. Therefore, strategy matters, but a clear strategy is necessary for success. It is not sufficient for *survival*. The right thing to worry about is execution, decisiveness, follow through, and delivering on commitments.

Knowledge Management

The management of intellectual capital has become a source of competitive advantage. For example, strategic approach to patents and tangible know-how such as trade secrets and technical expertise are identified as best practices and core competencies for an organization. Those would be categorized and effectively communicated internally. Some of the challenges in creating, developing, and documenting knowledge were described by a developer at Ernst & Young: "If people want to share, they are not going to do it even if you have the best technology in the world. People won't share if they don't see what's in it for them." A knowledge base without incentive and maintenance is worth nothing. The approach to developing knowledge bases is by developing modules of knowledge for different assemblies to fit specific applications. Changes in performance and incentive systems are essential to create a culture in which sharing is the norm. People have to feel and trust that they complement each other. The key is that performers must be convinced that their recognition comes from the mechanics of their project execution. The team members will recognize contribution, and the leader will automatically emerge.

Hedging

Hedges are complex transactions that are ways to contain losses if a stock declines, while still keeping some upside potential if the stock price keeps rising. Hedging, though, reduces an executive exposure to stock price drops in a way that investors have a hard time detecting. These complex transactions are structured such that executives still own the shares. Although hedges are announced at the time of inception, disclosures are often obscure in footnotes of public filings.

There are typically two major approaches to hedging: (1) zero cost collars, whereby there is a low and high limit across potential range of stock value and (2) the prepaid variable forward contract.

In the first approach, the executive would want to protect a certain number of shares at current market value. He buys a "put option" from a collaborating broker that gives him the right to sell the stock at defined lower value. To pay for the put option, he simultaneously sells a "call option," which allows the buyer to acquire the shares at a set price higher than current value. The executive holds on to his shares for the life of the agreement, and can also borrow funds generally at up to 50 percent of the value of the shares.

In the second approach, a more complex prepaid value forward contract is executed such that for a definite period, a low and high stock limit is established. The executive can receive up to 85 percent of the stock value at the time of contract. To protect itself, the investment bank usually shorts the company shares and charges fees on the contract. At the end of the contract time, the executive surrenders the number of stock specified in the contract to the bank, but keeps the cash paid upfront if the stock was selling for lower than the low limit. If the stock was trading at higher than the high limit, the executive can negotiate with the bank to keep the stock and benefit from the higher stock value. Alternatively, he can pay the investment bank back in stock; the exact number of shares depends on stock trading value. The better the stock value during the hedge contract period, the fewer shares will be owned by the executive. This approach allows the executive to free up more cash without initially selling his stock and paying capital gains tax.

In general, the hedge business helps investment bankers to cement ties with top company executives and bring lucrative fees to the banks. Nonetheless, the poor performance following hedging suggests that a number of these trades are potentially a conflict of interest based on privileged information by the executives. Officials might contest that the executives are trying to protect themselves against losses based on specific material information that the company performance had stumbled or just about to go negative that could potentially bring insider-trading charges against the executives at play having any material nonpublic information regarding the stock.

In conclusion, it is very difficult to know exactly what is behind any individual trades by looking at public filings. Many executives hedge to diversify holdings against their company shares. Typically, they diversify investment portfolio to realize liquidity and provide funding against charitable contributions and pledges.

Through hedging, we want to minimize exposure to exchange rates fluctuations. Goal is to protect investment by avoiding risk with forward contracts. Typically, hedging is used as a risk management tool to protect expected dollar value of a certain amount of monies exchanged, such as euro, yen, Yuan, Swiss Frank, English Pound, Saudi Riyal, etc. in a period. We want to minimize the risk of the exchange rate by transferring the risk on a price decline to others. A letter of credit (LC) could restrict receiving cash immediately, thereby creating the need to protect against any decrease in value. We are able to divide our risk through dynamic and static hedging. We can purchase put options to limit the risk on a down turn by drawing a contract to sell at a predetermined strike price, and preserve the chance to profit in a market appreciation. In addition, we might want to purchase a collar of a put option to protect against declines during the sale of a call option. This would offset the cost of the put option.

We need to intervene to minimize float—that is, the transit time of payments. Since there is an LC, the importer might balk at paying cash, but the bank that opens it is standing behind the money and the only check we need to do is the credit reputation of this issuing bank. Our preference would be for an irrevocable LC.

In managing exposure to risk through hedging, there are costs and benefits involved. If devaluation is unlikely, hedging may be a costly and inefficient way of doing business. If devaluation is expected, then the cost of using hedging techniques might be used to the extent that we can forecast future exchange rates.

Table 10.1   Currency Buying and Selling Options

Depreciation	Appreciation
Sell local currency forward	Buy local currency forward
Buy a local currency put option	Buy a local currency call option

As we are expecting cash inflow in months' period, then the forward rate needs to exceed its estimate of the future spot rate. Basic hedging techniques are included in table 10.1.

Like forward contracts, futures contracts must be settled at maturity. By contrast, currency options give the owner the right but not the obligation to buy (call option) or sell (put option) the contracted currency. A US option can be exercised at any time up to expiration date; a European option can be exercised only at maturity. For example, if the spot price of the euro in 90 days is $1.2, the forward contract gain is $2,000,000 \times [1.2-1.14])$ or 120, 000 euros. The amount by which the option is in-the-money represents its intrinsic value. Its time value represents the amount by which the price of the contract exceeds its intrinsic value. The call option is positively affected by an increase in time of expiration, volatility, and interest rate differential.

In a forward market hedge, a company that is long-a-foreign-currency will sell the foreign currency forward, whereas a company that is short-a-foreign- currency will buy the currency forward. In this way, the company can fix the dollar value of future foreign currency cash flow.

Hedging a particular currency exposure means establishing an offsetting currency position so that whatever is lost or gained on the capital currency exposure is exactly offset by corresponding foreign exchange gain or loss on the currency hedge. The three basic types of exposure are translation, transaction, and operating exposures. These exposures cannot always be neatly separated, but instead they overlap to a certain extent.

Translation exposure (accounting exposure) arises from the need of reporting, and consolidation of financial statements of foreign operations from the local currencies involved to the home currency. If the exchange rate has changed, then this translation or restatement of those assets, liabilities, revenues, expenses, gains, and losses will be affected.

Transaction exposure rises from known contractual binding future currency transactions (inflows or outflows). Since exchange rates vary, these transactions might have gains or losses. Although transaction exposure is part of economic exposure, it is usually lumped under accounting exposure. For example, currency-dominated accounts receivables and debt are included in the accounting exposure because they appear on the balance sheet. Other elements such as incomplete foreign currency sale (receivables are not created) do not appear on current financial statement; instead is part of operating expenses.

Operating exposure measures the extent to which currency fluctuations alter future cash flow. Therefore, any company whose cost is affected by currency changes has operating exposure. Both cash flow exposures and operating and transaction exposures combined equal the company's economic exposure. Therefore, economic exposure is the extent to which the value of the firm will change because of exchange rates change based on expected cash flow values.

Money Exchange

Real exchange rate change affects many aspects of the firm's operations and exposure. Price flexibility is important whereby the company can maintain its dollar margins both at home and abroad. The flexibility of the firm is measured by the ability in lowering or raising prices either to face lower priced imports or to raise its foreign currency-selling price to preserve profit margins.

The price elasticity of demand determines price flexibility, whereby a company may respond to exchange rates fluctuations. Differentiated products allow the firm to face competition both at home and abroad. Conversely, the less differentiated a company is, the harder it will face diversified competitors. These companies face the greatest amount of exchange risks.

The growth of offshore banking has been higher than domestic banking for the past two decades. This is primarily due to the growth in multinational operations and international diversification and globalization of business operations around the world. These operations created a multitude of contracts such as forward rate agreements that are cash-settled and the money had to be deposited in the various offshore banks where these operations might be taking place. Euro–dollar futures became more applicable, whereby a cash-settled contract for a specified period is based on deposits that pay London Interbank Offered Rate (LIBOR). Euro-dollar contracts are usually traded on quarterly basis. Contracts could be traded out to three years, with a high degree of liquidity out to two years. These levels of liquidity required additional banking transactions that were carried out offshore.

Although dwarfed by its European counterpart, the Asian dollar currency market has been growing in terms of both size and range of services provided. The Asian currency markets, for example, Singapore, offered lack of restrictive financial controls and taxes. This market was created as a satellite market to channel to the euro-dollar market the large pool of offshore funds since about 1968, mainly US dollars, circulating in Asia. This market provides for growth in South East Asia and provides deposit facilities for investors with excess funds. Asia Development bank issued the first dragon bond in 1991.

The growth of the international capital market, specifically the euro currency and Euro bond markets, is largely a response to the restrictions, regulations, and costs that governments impose on domestic financial transactions. At the same time, capital flows between the international markets and domestic markets have linked in a manner to minimize government interventions. For example, the use of interest rate and currency swaps. As Eurobonds became more viable, banks issued euro notes for their customers; nonunderwritten euro notes (Euro-commercial paper) is another innovation in the euro markets, which took money offshore.

The governments involved set a fixed exchange rate value. Market forces, on the other hand, set floating currency value. An exchange rate is simply the price of one nation's currency in terms of another currency, often termed as the reference currency. Exchange rate can be for spot or forward delivery. This depends on whether the currency is needed immediately or at some times in the future.

To understand how currency exchange rates are set, it helps to recognize that they are market-clearing prices that equilibrate supply and demand in foreign exchange markets. The demand and impact of exchange rate on the multinational corporations (MNCs), for example, drives the US demand for German goods and services. An increase in the euro's dollar value is equivalent to an increase in the dollar price of German products. Conversely, if the dollar value of the euro falls, Americans will demand more euros to buy less-expensive German products resulting in a downward demand for the euro.

The international monetary system refers to institutions and policies that determine the rate at which currency is exchanged. In a free float, as economic parameters change, market participants will adjust their current and future currency needs based on supply and demand until equilibrium is reached. A freely floating exchange rate system is usually referred to as a clean float. Exchange rate uncertainty reduces economic efficiency such that if exchange rates fluctuations were excessive, the central banks would intervene to smooth out and manage these fluctuations, thus, manage float or dirty float notation. The fixed rate system involves resisting fundamental upward or downward exchange rate movements for reasons unrelated to the exchange rates market.

Under a fixed rate system, governments are committed to managing target exchange rates. Each central bank buys or sells its currency whenever its exchange rate threatens to deviate from its stated par value. Usually this requires that all member nations have the same inflation rate, which is regulated through monetary policy. Floating rates absorb the pressures that would otherwise build up in countries that try to peg the exchange rate while simultaneously pursuing an independent monetary policy. For example, the Asian currency crisis did not spill over to Australia and New Zealand because the latter countries had floating exchange rates.

Through dollarization, currency boards, and monetary union, nations can fix their exchange rate. For example, the European Central bank for countries using the Euro control for monetary independence of the members, and the Federal Reserve for countries such as Ecuador and Panama that have dollarized.

MNCs

The strategies followed by the MNCs in hedging currency market limitations rely on product innovation, product differentiation, or some other cartels or collusion to protect themselves from competitive threats. The value of international diversification will enable MNCs to supply currency benefits through selling or buying depending whether the currency in that market is fixed or floating. Decisions are usually made to take advantage of currency movements and exchange rate to benefit the investors. They can easily do that through consolidation of financial statements by moving a transaction from one exposure to another.

Evidence in operating profits of MNCs suggests that corporations should continue investing abroad. The recommended approach for additional foreign risk is to estimate the cost of capital in comparison to risk at a relative capital investment domestically. The typical result of using the global version of the Capital Assets Pricing Model (CAPM) is to estimate a lower cost of equity than when in the US (home) market as the benchmark. The optimal global capital structure entails a mix of debt and equity for the parent entity. Affiliate capital structure should vary to take advantage of opportunities that would minimize cost of capital. MNCs might benefit from below-market financing in one market to finance other operations elsewhere.

MNCs could use triangular currency arbitrage to create additional monies to reduce cost of capital employed on a project. Other methods of creative financing can be used to achieve various objectives, such as lowering cost of funds. They may use structured notes, which are complex debt instruments whose payments are tied to a reference index, such as LIBOR, and that might have embedded derivative elements. These measures would allow MNCs to function more efficiently by tailoring the cost of capital needed to an individual project.

The cost of capital is the minimum risk-adjusted required rate of return by shareholders. The cost of equity capital for a firm is the minimum rate that would induce investors to buy, or hold, the firm's stock. The weighted average cost of capital for foreign projects must have marginal weights that reflect the firm's target capital structure. The project systemic risk or beta coefficient is a factor that determines the risk premium associated with the project. Key issues in estimating foreign discounts on cost of capital are:

- Should corporate proxies be U.S. or foreign entities?
- Is the project risk estimated based on proxy betas of US, local, or international portfolio?
- What is the risk premium based on—US, local, or international market?
- How is the country risk incorporate in the cost of capital estimates?

A global CAPM would be an appropriate model to use with implications to the MNCs. Benefits included in a globally integrated market is that investors are able to reduce some of the risk that they would have to bear in an otherwise segmented market.

In estimating the weighted average cost of capital for an MNC or its affiliates, the capital structure should be the outcome of an optimal financial plan. The focus should be on the worldwide capital structure because suppliers of capital are assumed to associate the risk of a default on a worldwide debt ratio. The earnings diversification provided by foreign operations might enable the MNC to leverage more highly than purely domestic firms without increasing default risk.

The International Fisher Effect (IFE) states that the interest differential between two countries should be an unbiased predictor of the future change in the spot rate. For example, through a forward contract, which might be set up today using a derivative instrument such as an option, IFE would predict currency values.

The key to understanding the impact of relative changes in nominal interest rates among countries on the foreign exchange rate of a currency is to evaluate implications of purchasing power parity. Therefore, exchange rates will move to offset changes in inflation rate differentials. A rise in US inflation will mean a decline in the USD value or a rise in US interest rate.

In effect, the IFE says that currencies with low interest rates are expected to appreciate relative to currencies with high interest rates. Therefore, if we want to compare the USD to the euro based on the current value for a period of one year, assuming the expected euro interbank interest rate is 2.26 percent, the expected Federal funds will be at 1.25 percent, practically, 1 percent differential, (e.g., $1 = 0.746 euros); we expect the dollar to rise against the euro by about 1 percent or we expect that $1 = 0.739 euros a year from current value.

A brief examination of the dollar's fluctuations provides further insight into the relation of exchange rate movements. In the early 1980s, tax rates and inflation rate were sharply reduced; economic growth accelerated to 6.5 percent in 1984. Capital was attracted to the United States and the dollar rose sharply. As the US growth slowed down in 1985 and foreign growth accelerated the world decreased holding assets in the United States, it created a portfolio rebalance. The dollar fell.

The desire to hold a currency today depends critically on expectations of factors that can affect the currency future value. Japanese automakers have protected themselves against a rising yen by purchasing a significant percentage of intermediate components from independent suppliers. This practice called outsourcing gives them the flexibility to shift purchases of intermediate inputs toward suppliers with costs least affected by exchange rate changes. Some of these inputs come from South Korea or Taiwan, which are linked to the US dollar. Thus, even if these goods are not priced in dollars, the yen-equivalent prices tend to decline with the dollar, thereby, lessen the impact of a falling dollar on the cost of Japanese cars sold in the United States. Japan historically has resisted revaluation of the yen for fear of its consequences for Japanese exports with unofficial pegging. Japan linked their currency in a target zone system, where they can adjust their economic policies to maintain their exchange rates within a specific margin around agreed-upon and fixed central exchange rates.

Government-industry cooperation, a strong work ethics, mastery of high technology, and a comparatively small defense allocation (1% of GDP) have helped Japan advance with extraordinary rapidity to the rank of second most technologically powerful economy in the world after the United States and third largest economy in the world after the United States and China. One notable characteristic of the economy is the working together of manufacturers, suppliers, and distributors in closely knit groups called Keiretsu. There is a question mark about the effectiveness of these Keiretsus on the overall performance of the economy. A second basic feature has been the guarantee of lifetime employment for a substantial portion of the urban labor force. Both features are now eroding. The industrial sector, which is the most important sector of the economy, is heavily dependant on imported raw materials and fuels. The much smaller agricultural sector is highly subsidized and protected. However, the crop yields are among the highest in the world. Although self-sufficient in rice, Japan must import over 50 percent of its grain and other fodder crops. Japan has a large fishing fleet that accounts for 15 percent of global catch.

For three decades, overall real economic growth had been spectacular: 10 percent average in the 1960s, 5 percent average in the 1970s, and 4 percent in the 1980s. Nevertheless, growth slowed markedly in the 1990s largely because of the aftereffects of overinvestment during the late 1980s, and contractionary domestic policies intended to wring speculative growth have met with little success and were further hampered in 2000–02 by the slowing of the US and Asian economies. The crowding of habitable land area and the aging of the population are two major problems. Robotics constitutes a key long-term economic strength, with Japan possessing 57 percent of the world total. The yen exchange rate and value fluctuations had followed the above description closely; however, the internal conflict over the approach and proper means to reform the banking system, which is ailing, appear to continue.

11

Conclusions and Future Recommendations

Key questions are—How do we get people committed to a new vision? How do we motivate people to line up? They must feel and believe that they have a piece of the pie! People will help you implement the change and might go with you for a while, but they must also grab part of the gain. Even simple recognitions will go a long way. Financial gains are also very motivating. Being part of a winning team that produces results that are tangible and meaningful is very motivating. People want to be part of something that really works.

The mechanism of going in circles against spiral build up to spring a forward change and progress through centrifugal (centripetal) forces is the key to maintain momentum in a process. One needs to increase build up of activities through speed and evade status quo. The team would concentrate on deep understanding versus bravado. The confrontation of the realities of things versus embracing fads develops consistent behavior against erratic decisions. The culture of discipline vis-à-vis anarchy utilizes scientific approach to defeat unfounded concepts. Cause and effect relationships versus just because acceptance is key in determining the selection of team members with common sense; select the right people versus fill the place with hot bodies; select leaders versus bureaucrats; use data and results versus defined positions. Develop people with results orientation versus not being fully focused and engaged in the required tasks that lead to projects completion. Refine the team based on keeping the right people and getting rid of the wrong people. Accelerate simple fast processes, prepare, and train people for desired goals and results.

Besides making money, the ability to stimulate and preserve core competence and propel progress is key to the future of the organization. Defining clear and realistic objectives that are achievable is a very important healthy course of action for the success of a company.

Main Values

The following characteristics should be embodied by employees of a progressive organization:

- technical contribution;
- respect for individuals;
- responsibility and accountability; and
- that profit should be an outcome of doing things right, not the major focus.

A company exists for what it provides, rather than how much it makes in sales or profit (these values should be results of the reason for existence). The lifeblood of the company is its customers, not its profit. As you build customers, profits will grow, as Merck & Co believes: "Medicine is for the patient, profit follows."

As Jim Collins (2001) said in "Good to Great"—"First Who…Then What…" When you care about doing meaningful work and your responsibilities take you along this path, your life will be meaningful and you will achieve deep satisfaction knowing that your time is well spent and what you do matters.

Traits of high achievers such as the superior CEO are described below:

1. Integrity, maturity, energy (foundation of everything else).
2. Business acumen: a deep understanding of the business and a strong profit orientation—an almost instinctive feel for how the company makes money.
3. People acumen: judging, leading teams, growing and coaching people, cutting losses where necessary.
4. Organizational acumen: engendering trust, sharing information, listening expertly; diagnosing whether the organization is performing at full potential; delivering on commitments; changing, not just running the business; being decisive and incisive.
5. Curiosity, intellectual capacity, global mindset. Being extremely oriented and hungry for global knowledge; adept at connecting developments and spotting patterns.
6. Superior judgment.
7. An insatiable appetite for accomplishments and results.
8. Powerful motivation to grow and convert learning into practice.
9. People first, strategy second. Strategy is only half the battle.

Strategic Planning

Choosing ends such as goals are described as dreams with deadlines. These audacious goals develop ways and critical paths. They emphasize milestones including small steps. Strategic leaps with the logic of ends–ways–means define marketing in terms of: segmentation, targeting, and positioning. The language we use to describe our world has a profound influence on how we perceive it, and it goes a long way to fashioning our attitudes, motivations, and ultimately the choice of our actions. A company culture implies values, convention such as aggressiveness, defensiveness, nimbleness. It sets a pattern for a company activities, opinions, and actions. A company culture can be its major strength when it is consistent with its strategies.

Inventory systems

Inventory is the stock of any item or resource in an organization. These can include raw materials, finished products, component parts, supplies, and work in process. An inventory system is the set of policies and controls that monitor levels and determines what levels should be maintained, when stock should be replenished, and when orders are placed. The purpose of inventory is to maintain independence of operations, meet variations in product demand, satisfy customer requirements, allow flexibility in production schedule, provide safeguard against any variation in raw materials deliveries, and take advantage of economic purchases. The optimized order quantity is a direct relationship with holding cost, annual cost of item, and ordering cost. The total annual cost is directly proportional to demand, cost per unit, and holding and storage inventory cost per unit. Just-in-time (JIT) can be defined as an integrated set of activities designed to achieve high volume production using minimal inventories. It also involves the elimination of waste. (Lean process is a JIT process). The evolution of Enterprise Resource Planning (ERP) systems has been driven by the emergence of new business practices and information technology. This has been supported by growth and maturing manufacturing operations and commercially developed software packages.

Supply Chain

Supply chain management, customer relationship management, just-in-time and lean manufacturing, are all examples of developed business practices including e-commerce.

Supply chain management synchronizes supplies with demands and responds to change. An ERP system provides the tools to manage scenarios from simple to complex to meet customer-changing requirements in a very flexible manner. The simple model is based on items acquisition from suppliers and in turn, produces items for direct sales to customers internally. The ERP systems handle the buy-or-make items for these operations. In the complex model, the enterprise buys from external suppliers, authorized dealers/distributors and other manufacturing plants. It focuses on coordinating delivery of the required items from a single or multiple sources based on actual availability and most optimal lead-time. It would initiate subcontracts based on additional requirements to satisfy customer demands to satisfy a variable schedule. This complex ERP system sells and ships products directly to customers through multisales channels, such as resellers, distributors, or OEMs. This also involves multisites with inventory and distribution centers replenished from manufacturing plants based on demands. Sales orders can be satisfied based on available inventory across the distribution network. Items might also be drop-shipped from a supplier or a subcontract site. Supply chain management concepts intersects with customer-oriented strategies and e-commerce.

The use of information technology has facilitated customer relations. For example, the use of portable computers makes it feasible for a sales representative to analyze data in the field using ERP applications during face-to-face meetings for a quick response. The representative can define customer requirements and suggest appropriate products, or create a quote for a custom production configuration.

Cheap Labor Markets

The effects of China's rising wages and undervalued stronger currency are rippling through the small business markets such as the textile and garment makers. This wage increase is challenging the future of business success all across China by creating pressure to cope with higher costs. Wages are creeping upward on annual basis. This has adversely created pressures on multinationals such as Toyota and Honda motors, and national companies such as Hon Hai Precision industry Co., which is one of the world's biggest contract manufacturers of electronic components with increased wages of up to 30 percent.

The small business clusters, which account for 60 percent of the economy and about 80 percent of the job market, for example, bamboo and shoes products of Huizhou, cigarette lighters of Wenzhou, silk from Suzhou, and children's clothing from Zhili, they all are reliant on low-cost labor that is increasingly in short supply.

The effects of currency appreciation by up to 10 percent would create a more difficult cost advantage for China's products. That is why the Chinese government, despite outside pressure, is generally expected to limit the pace of currency appreciation.

Leadership Traits

- Foster McGaw:

"Hire no one you wouldn't invite to your family's dining table"

- Jim Collins in *Good to Great*:

"First, determine who gets on the bus"

Table 11.1 draws a contrast between leaders and managers.

Table 11.1   Characteristics of Leaders against Managers

Leaders	Managers
Challenge status quo	Accept status quo
Trust	Control
Innovate / develop	Administer / maintain
Ask What / Why	Ask When / How
Do the right things	Do things right
Watch the horizon	Watch the bottom line

Leadership is a matter of Intelligence, Trustworthiness, Humaneness, Courage, and Discipline...Reliance on Intelligence alone results in Rebelliousness. Exercising Humaneness alone results in Weakness. Fixation on Trust results in Folly. Dependence on the Strength of Courage results in Violence. Exercising discipline as sternness in command results in Cruelty. When one has all five Virtues together, each appropriate to its function, and then one can be a Leader....

Sun Tzu,

(The Art of War ...Better Then, the Art of Winning...)

Table 11.2   Value Proposition—World Class

We make it happen
We provide access to high quality.
We help transform systems.
We are the world's leading company.
We are committed to delivering innovative specialty to market.

We do the right thing
We strive for preeminence in the development, manufacturing, and
  marketing of products and services.
We are committed to the safety of our employees and the quality of our
  products.
We deliver on our promises.
We demonstrate and expect honesty, integrity, and mutual respect.

We lead the way
We empower everyone to add value.
We seize opportunities.
We are bold. We set the pace.
We step up and take charge.
We embrace change.
We grow through reinvention, innovation, and continuous improvement.

We drive for results
We have a passion for customer satisfaction.
We are responsible to our shareholders, customers, and communities.
We are successful because of our employees.
We have high expectations.

You make the difference
We are proud.
We make quality products accessible together.

Table 11.2 enlists the main values that are important in developing a world-class organization.

Being equipped with moral programming does not mean we practice moral behavior and empathy. Something still has to boot up the program / software and configure it properly. That something is usually the team. The basic sense of ethical equivalent is just as syntax is nothing until words are built upon it. The sense of right or wrong and empathy are similarly structured and based on the team being able to teach on how to apply these principles.

Leadership Practices

Choose to invite exceptional people to coin an exceptional culture and make a difference. The main characteristics in these exceptional people should focus on what mettle they possess. What is their drive? How much intellectual capacity they have? What is the level of their knowledge and expertise?

The mettle is the measure of integrity, courage, honor, and ethics. The drive metric is based on pride, craftsmanship, strong desire to make a difference, and passion. Intellectual capacity gauges intelligence, judgment, fairness, tough-mindedness, empathy, and tough skin. Finally, knowledge and expertise will trace experience, education, and curiosity.

The driving philosophy is spearheaded to combine all fundamentals with innovative practices and technologies to serve all constituents. The focus of leadership should be on local leadership, as there is no substitute to local leadership. Local leadership prospers in open organizations and vanishes when power is concentrated. The question is: why is power so dangerous? The issue with power is that it corrupts; exceptional people resent arbitrary decisions and exceptional managers avoid them. Power is the tool of the insecure: It is a reflection of persons who enlarge themselves like a puffer fish. It corrupts the elitist, the opportunist, and the less-skilled. Destructive forms of power include displays of edicts, usurpation, and ones that drive a wedge; such practices can hurt everyone. How does a wedge destroy trust?

Driving a wedge manipulates partial disclosures, misrepresentations, means justifying the end, claims of righteousness, assuming the victim role, and attempting to lead without following. Avoiding the power traps start by recognizing that power corrupts. One should always look for options as they beat taking a position. A leader will always look to include and elevate a situation seeking cooperation.

Why is interdependence helpful? Everyone starts out as dependent and most become independent. Leaders achieve interdependence; the ability to confidently ask others to help. The analogy for leaders is on how scouts and renegades differ. Renegades ride, while scouts, as leaders, ride to care. The scout propels the group forward. There is no leadership from behind. There is no leadership in being in the lead and unaware of conditions behind.

The judiciary aspect of management is governed by the fact that exceptional managers and judges have common traits: excellent listening skills, objectivity, honesty, impartiality, and fairness. In addition, awareness of precedents, multiples, tough-mindedness, and respect for the rules. Leaders choose to disclose all news and bad news the fastest. Team members need the assurance that they are secure in soaking up and getting heard. It is better to disagree and discuss than to agree on the wrong course. Team members must learn to leave the room with one heart. Peacemakers remember to be positive even under adverse conditions. Peacemakers cement team relations and strengthen resolve. Hidden agendas eventually consume credibility and trust. Dysfunctional organizations often suffer internal fiefdoms and infighting. Fiefdoms tend to emerge in authoritative organizations where assigning blame is a big advantage; when metrics are inadequate, rewards are arbitrary. The obligation of leaders is to avoid isolation, favoritism, wedges, and act like master of ceremonies in a parade. Leaders need to recognize that organizations are not hard-wired. Organizations provide talent, capability, and capital for a vision or objective; unfortunately, organizations can also concentrate power. The ideal organization avoids concentration of power and raises performance standards way above average. A cultivating organization where everyone counts, with respect and appreciation to all, where happy people excel, collective intelligence reduces risk, and consultative style prevails. In such organizations, exceptional people know how to replace large egos with mutual respect; they love to mentor motivated employees and recognize the ones who strive for accomplishments in a team cooperative environment.

Exceptional people deserve and require exceptional growth. They exhibit a commitment to learning and un-learning. They take control of situations and support their team. They tend to have the ability to integrate; they establish mutual trust with fellow managers and put respect ahead of popularity. In business, being average eventually brings losses. The sustainability of a business is tied to its above-average elements. As the burden with dealing with average increases, leaders who accept average have a difficult time winning. Excellent managers differentiate between helping people succeed and helping people.

Leaders may enter a comfort zone where strengths can be overdone; arrogance replaces confidence, big ego takes over high self-esteem, impulsiveness overshadows bias for action, and lone wolf covers individuality; thin skin replaces sensitivity;

mothering takes over caring; and controlling substitutes being in control.

As we look forward, we can compare context to core values. Activities, which are context in nature, tend to accumulate and seldom go away on their own and without consequences. The litmus test is governed by the question: If we want to cut back, which things would we do without? We should not be impressed with perfect slates; those who draw the target around the arrow. We recognize that high performers hold themselves to higher standards and always demand maximum performance. They tend to be harder on themselves, while treating others gently. Finally, as we focus on managerial tools, one needs to differentiate between events and processes. Are there risks in confusing the two? We need to ask, how do we determine whether a situation is a simple event or the result of a process? How do we detect a bad process? In managerial terms, we need to check for rot. Rot is weakness. Below the surface, we need to test for rot, determine the cause of rot, and address the rot.

Continuous Improvement

People recognize that in order to survive and continue to grow adopting a culture of continuous improvement is a necessity. A quality improvement method such as Six Sigma is one of the most widely used approaches today. Manufacturing technologies refer to "lean" as a discipline that focuses the process on cycle time reduction and elimination of waste through effectiveness improvement utilizing these statistical techniques.

Continuous improvement requires a dedication to study data to identify and eliminate process problems. Indeed, along this road, a set of polices and procedures start to evolve to create process control. The benefit of all this is that the organization starts to generate positive results in their day-to-day business.

The broader framework will translate into meeting company's goals and customer needs.

One of the key foundations to improve processes is to eliminate variation. "Everything varies. What is important is that the way in which something varies; the patterns in the variation can expose the cause of problems and point the way towards solutions" (George et al., 2005). Therefore, fixing the process will create improvement levels. Improving process flow and speed is one significant goal that has underlying variations as most common sources of problems. Significant interactions of the main process variables are important in understanding why the process is not in control. Therefore, examining how workflows are followed is critical. Accordingly, basing decisions on data and facts are at the cornerstones of continuous improvement methodologies. In addition, people have to work together to make the kind of improvements that customers will notice.

Besides lead-time, value-added and non–value-added work needs to be fully understood and quantified. This will lead to all waste elimination. Some waste is inevitable as methods cannot be 100 percent effective. Albeit process complexities, which might entail many products, services, options, features that need to be considered in an evaluation of process improvement, the focus should be on simplification and tackling the key significant interactions that are influencing the process in a major way.

When companies start using lean methods, they usually create special programs that create new staff positions, expand responsibilities of some existing positions, develop appropriate training for one involved, and set up procedures to make sure that the efforts are linked to important business issues. The terms champions, black belts, master black belts, start to appear among the staff positions. Green belts, yellow belts, white belts, and team members can be anyone in the organization who receives some level of awareness education or skill training on "Six Sigma." Ultimately, it is significant for these programs to work if they are linked to business priorities. This new infrastructure helps companies translate their investment in "lean six sigma" into measurable results, by tracing the metrics of improvement to the organization and its customers.

To make improvements that last, a Define–Measure–Analyze– Improve–Control (DMAIC) process is usually structured as a data-based problem-solving process. This means doing specific activities in a specific sequence, gathering data in every phase to make decisions, and making sure that the solutions implemented will really eliminate the cause of the problem at hand. Another technique is the Suppliers-Input–Process-Output-Customers (SIPOC) diagram, which focuses on reducing the number of errors in orders and corresponding invoices, for example. It targets to identify the basic elements of the process and also critical-to-quality (CTQ) indicators. The value stream map, based on an actual process, captures the main sequence of activities. Typically, notations show wait time (delays) and rework loops (waste).

Data collection starts with process observations. Following, measurement tools such as Pareto charts, time series plots, cause-and-effect diagrams, scatter plots, pick charts are useful to graph the data and evaluate trends. Control charts are useful to reflect on where the process is out-of-control. It takes discipline to find real solutions to problems. The DMAIC framework provides that discipline and structure to teams. Hence, it is a scientific approach to make improvements that last.

In conclusion, to create and maintain an organized, clean, safe, and high performance workplace, the term 5S (Sort, Set-in-order, Shine, Standardize, Sustain) was coined. 5S enables to distinguish between normal and abnormal conditions at a glance (George et al., 2005). 5S is the foundation of continuous improvement, zero defects, cost reduction, and safe work place area. It is a systematic way to improve the workplace, processes, and products through all employees' involvement in this order: alternatively sort–simplify–sweep–standardize–sustain. To sort is to clearly distinguish needed items from unneeded ones and eliminate those that are not needed. To simplify is to set in order and keeping items in the correct place to allow for easy and immediate retrieval. To sweep or shine is to keep items clean and work area swept. Standardization is the key to repeat quality in terms of products or processes. It allows meeting the same expectations each time a product is made or a process is repeated. Sustaining is a display of self-discipline whereby it is habitual to maintain established procedures. The use and implementation of the 5S is a way of cultural control in an organization, as you cannot control the business only through numbers, but more through the orderly discipline of established processes.

Glossary

BSC   Balanced Scorecard.

BTO   Build-to-order, a manufacturing strategy that builds products only after the receipt of an order for those products.

Channel   Sales and distribution network.

ERP   Enterprise Resource Planning, which describes large-scale, integrated software systems designed to manage all or a large portion of a company's operations and support functions.

EVA   Economic Value Added, a measure of profitability that identifies net income beyond that which provides a market return to the shareholders.

IT   Information Technology.

JIT   Just-in-time, an inventory management technique that attempts to time receipts of raw materials to make them available when needed for production but not earlier.

PC   Personal computer.

ROA   Return on Assets (net income plus interest expense divided by average total assets).

ROE   Return on Equity (net income divided by average shareholders' equity).

SAP   Systems Applications Program, an ERP software product of SAP AG.

S&P   The Standard and Poor's listing of 500 largest companies.

VAR   Value-Added Reseller, a channel firm that takes products from the original manufacturer and adds its own service or integrates other products and then markets a more comprehensive product to the end user.

References

Bliss, Jeff, and Jerry Rosa. (October 6, 1997) "Waitt Weighs in on Channel and Corporate Battle Plans." *Computer Reseller News*, issue 757.

Brynjolfsson, Erik, and Lorin Hitt. (October 1997) "Information Technology and Organizational Design: Some Evidence from Micro Data." MIT Working Paper.

Compaq Computer Corporation. (1998a) *1997 Annual Report*. Houston, TX: Compaq Computer Corporation.

——. (1998b) *SEC 10K Report*. Houston, TX: Compaq Computer Corporation.

——. (June 12, 1998c) "Compaq CEO Pfeiffer Unveils Company Strategy." Compaq Computer Corporation Press Release.

Cunningham, Cara, and Ed Scannell. (July 10, 1997) "Compaq Executive Brass Tout New, Three-Phase Distribution Model." *InfoWorld Electric*.

Damore, Kelley, and Brian Gillooly. (March 21, 1994) "Compaq Reorganizes U.S. Operations." *Computer Reseller News*.

Davenport, Thomas H. (1997) *Information Ecology*. New York: Oxford University Press.

Dell Computer Corporation. (1998) *SEC 10K Report*. Round Rock, TX: Dell Computer Corporation.

Farre, Tom. (January 1, 1996) "Compaq Pushes Beyond the PC." *VARBusiness Magazine*, issue 1201.

——. (May 15, 1997) "Compaq Reengineers Again." *VARBusiness Magazine*, issue 1308.

Frank, Diane. (July 8,1996) "Compaq Reorganizes, Senior VP Stimac Resigns." *InfoWorld Electric*. http://www.infoworld.com.

Ferguson, Kevin. (September 22, 1997) "Gateway: Everything's Not So Black and White." *Computer Retail Week*, issue 183.

Gateway Computer Corporation. (1998) *SEC 10K Report*. North Sioux City, SD: Gateway Computer Corporation.

Gillooly, Caryn, and Mary E. Thyfault. (October 10, 1994) "Practicing What They Preach." *InformationWeek*. http://www.informationweek.com.

Girishankar, Saroja. (August 11, 1997) "Compaq Builds Global Transaction System." *Communications Week.* http://www.communicationsweek.com.

Goldstein, Alan. (September 2, 1997) "Dell Computer Founder Looks for Ways to Stay Ahead of Pack." *Dallas Morning News.*

Hammer, Michael. (1990) "Reengineering Work: Don't Automate, Obliterate. *Harvard Business Review* 68 (4) (July/August): 104–112.

Hammer, Michael, and James Champy. (May 3, 1993) "Explosive Thinking." *Computerworld* 27 (18): 123–125.

Hoovers. (1998) "Hoovers Online." http://www.hoovers.com.

Infobeads. (1998) "The Sub $1000 PC Market Meets Its Match." Computer Intelligence. http://www.ci.infobeads.com/InfoBeads/.

Jordan, Peter. (October 15, 1996) "Compaq Reengineers Itself into Top Desktop Vendor." *VAR Business Magazine,* issue 1217.

Jubak, Jim. (August 25, 1998) "Dell vs. Compaq." Jubak's Journal, Microsoft Investor. http://investor.msn.com/prospect/articles/jubak.

Kane, Margaret. (October 27, 1997) "Domination—Compaq and Dell Surge." *ZDNN.* http://www.zdnet.comn/zdnn.

———. (April 27, 1998) "Inventory Woes Don't Slow PC Growth." *PC Week Online.* http://www.zdnet.com/pcweek.

Kanellos, Michael. (October 16, 1997) "Compaq Tests Web Sales Waters." *CNET.* http://www.cnet.com.

Kirkpatrick, David, and Sheree R. Curry. (April 1, 1996) "Fast Times at Compaq." *Fortune Magazine.*

Kaplan, Robert S., and David P. Norton. (1992) "The Balanced Scorecard—Measures That Drive Performance." *Harvard Business Review* (January/February): 71–79.

Kaplan, Robert S., and David P. Norton. (1996) *The Balanced Scorecard.* Boston, MA: Harvard Business School Press.

Lemos, Bob. (July 26, 1998) "Compaq Clear No.1 in Q2." *ZDNN.* http://www.zdnet.comn/zdnn.

Manzi, Jim. (May 4, 1992) "Productivity: Faith isn't Enough." *Computerworld* 26 (18): 29.

Mata, F. J., W. L. Fuerst, and J. B. Barney. (1995) "Information Technology and Sustained Competitive Advantage: A Resource-Based Analysis." *MIS Quarterly* 19 (4) (December): 487–505.

McGarvey, Joe. (July 9, 1997) "Compaq Thinks Big." *ZDNN Interactive Week.* http://www.zdnet.com/zdnn/content/inwk/.

McWilliams, Gary. (July 22, 1996) "Compaq at the Crossroads." *Business Week.*

Melymuka, Kathleen. (October 15, 1997) "Hewlett-Packard Wins and Digital Falls to Back of the Pack." *VAR Business Magazine.*

Mooney, J. G., V. Gurbaxani, and K. Kraemer. (1995) "A Process Oriented Framework for Assessing the Business Value of IT." *Proceedings of the 16th International Conference on Information Systems.* In J. I DeGross et al., eds. 10–13 December, 17–27 .

Nee, Eric. (January 12, 1998) "Compaq Computer Corp." *Forbes Magazine.*

NewsEdge Corporation. (1997) "Compaq Announces Record Third Quarter Sales, Earnings, and EVA." *NewsEdge Corporation.* http://www.newspage.com.

Planning Review. (1994) "Compaq Computer." *Bell PubliCom for the North American Society for Corporate Planning* 22 (July).

Porter, Michael E., and Victor E. Millar. (1985) "How Information Gives You Competitive Advantage." *Harvard Business Review* 63 (4) (July/August): 149–160.

Porter, Michael E. (1996) "What is Strategy?" *Harvard Business Review* 74 (6) (November/December): 61–78.

Slavin, Roy H. (1994) "Re-engineering: A Productivity Paradox." *Quality* 33 (6) (June): 18.

Schwartz, Ephraim, and Dan Briody. (October 27, 1997) "Compaq CEO Sets Goal of $50 Billion in Sales." *InfoWorld Electric.* http://www.infoworld.com.

Waurzyniak, Patrick. (January 27, 1998) "IDC Reports Healthy 14 Percent PC Growth." *Electronic Buyer's News.*

Wilcox, Joe. (June 26, 1998) "Compaq Cuts 5,000 in Facilities Consolidation." *Computer Reseller News.*

Wong, Wylie. (October 28, 1997) "Dataquest, IDC Q3 Figures Put Compaq atop of PC Sales Heap." *Computerworld Magazine Online.* http://www2/computerworld/com/home/.

Zlotnikov, Vladim. (November 3, 1997) "PC Sales Growth Remains Down." *Electronic Buyers News.*

Zuckerman, Laurence. (June 16, 1997) "Compaq: We're No. 1, but We Can Change." *New York Times—CyberTimes.* http://www.nytimes.com.

Bibliography

Collins, J. (2001). *Good to Great.* New York: Harper Collins.

Bossidy, L., and R. Charan. (2002). *Execution.* New York: Crown Business.

George, M. L., D. Rowlands, M. Price, and J. Maxey. (2005) *Lean Six Sigma Pocket Toolbook.* New York: McGraw-Hill.

Rayport, J., and J. Sviokla. (1994) "Managing in the Marketspace." *Harvard Business Review* (November/December): 141–150.

Rayport, J., and J. Sviokla. (1995) "Exploring the Virtual Value Chain." *Harvard Business Review* (November/December): 75–85.

Judge, P. C. (1998) "Are Tech Buyers Different?" *Business Week* (January 26): 64–65.

Yovovich, B. G. (1998) "Webbed Feat." *Marketing News* (January 19): 1, 18.

Sellers, P. (1989) "Getting Customers to Love You." *Fortune* (March 13): 38–49.

Porter, M. E. (1985) *Competitive Advantage. Creating and Sustaining Superior Performance.* New York: Free Press, Simon & Schuster.

Business Week. (1991) "Value Marketing: Quality, Service, and Fair Pricing are the Keys to Selling in the 90s." (November 11): 132–140.

Stewart, T. A. (1997) "A Satisfied Customer isn't Enough." *Fortune* (July 21): 112–113.

Lanning, M. J. (1998) *Delivering Profitable Value.* Oxford, UK: Capstone.

Kaplan, R. S., and D. P. Norton (1996) *The Balanced Score Card: Translating Strategy into Action.* Boston, MA: Harvard Business School Press.

Katzenbach, J. R., and D. K. Smith. (1993) *The Wisdom of Teams: Creating the High-Performance Organization.* Boston, MA: Harvard Business School Press.

Hammer, M., and J. Champy. (1993) *Reengineering the Corporation.* New York: Harper Business.

Garrett, E. M. (1994) "Outsourcing to the Max." *Small Business Reports*, August, 9–14.

Quinn, J. B. (1992) *Intelligent Enterprise.* New York: Free Press.

Prahalad, C. K., and G. Hamel. (1990) "The Core Competence of the Corporation." *Harvard Business Review* (May/June): 79–91.

Gitomer, J. (1998) *Customer Satisfaction Is Worthless, Customer Loyalty Is Priceless: How to Make Customers Love You, Keep Them Coming Back and Tell Everyone They Know.* Austin, TX: Bard Press.

Berry, L. L., and A. Parasuraman. (1991) *Marketing Services: Competing through Quality.* New York: Free Press, 136–142.

Cross, R., and J. Smith. (1995) *Customer Bonding: Pathways to Lasting Loyalty.* Lincolnwood, IL: NTC Business Books.

Business Week. (1982) "Quality: The U.S. Drives to Catch Up." November, 66–80.

Traffic Management. (1990) "The Gurus of Quality: American Companies are Heading the Quality Gospel Preached By Deming, Juran, Crosby, and Taguchi." (July): 35–39.

Miller, C. (1993) "U.S. Firms Lag in Meeting Global Quality Standards." *Marketing News*, February 15.

Bandura, A., and D. Cervone. (1986) "Social Foundations of Thought and Action." *Journal of Personality & Social Psychology* 45 (5): 1017.

Bandura, et al . (1992) *American Educational Research Journal* 29 (3): 663.

Elliott, Jaques. (1997) *Requisite Organization: Total System for Effective Managerial Organization and Managerial Leadership for the 21st Century*. London: Gower. ISBN 0–566–07940–2.

Sims, Henry P., and Peter Lorenzi. 1992 *The New Leadership Paradigm: Social Learning and Cognition in Organizations*. Newbury Park, CA: Sage Publications, Inc.

Bandura, A. (1977) *Social Learning Theory*. New York: General Learning Press.

Bandura, A. (1997) *Self-Efficacy: The Exercise of Control*. New York: Freeman.

Bandura, A. (1986) *Social Foundations of Thought and Action*. Englewood Cliffs, NJ: Prentice-Hall.

Bandura, Albert. (1997) "The Nature and Structure of Self-Efficacy." In *Self-Efficacy: The Exercise of Control*. New York: W. H. Freeman, 36–38.

Index

.

The manufacturer's authorised representative in the EU is Springer
Nature Customer Service Centre GmbH, Europaplatz 3, 69115 Heidelberg,
Germany. If you have any concerns regarding our products, please
contact ProductSafety@springernature.com

Printed and bound by CPI Group (UK) Ltd, Croydon, CR0 4YY

23/04/2026

02095595-0005